W9-AYE-986

POLYMER CLAY
mosaics

SUE HEASER

NORTH LIGHT BOOKS

cincinnati, ohio
www.artistsnetwork.com

about the author

▶▶ **Sue Heaser** is an English polymer clay designer and artist who has worked full-time in the medium since 1985. Initially she ran a small business making and supplying polymer clay jewelry to a large number of craft, fashion and gift outlets in eastern England. For the past seven years, she has been writing and illustrating articles and books on polymer clay, pushing the medium in ever-new directions.

After a globe-trotting childhood in the Far East, Middle East and Africa, Sue studied at Falmouth College of Art and Exeter University in England. She initially worked for the Museum of London and progressed to a career as an archaeological illustrator. Her studies of the ancient artifacts used in the arts and crafts of antiquity led her to develop skills in many crafts, and after her two daughters were born, she combined motherhood with freelance illustration, glass engraving, candle making and puppetry. In 1981 she discovered polymer clay, which has held her interest longer than anything else to date! She works in jewelry, miniatures, dolls, puppets, mosaics, fine art, simulations and many other genres that are ever increasing in number.

Sue's first major book, *Making Polymer Clay Jewellery*, was published in June 1997. Four more polymer clay books followed in quick succession: *Making Doll's House Miniatures with Polymer Clay*, *Making Miniature Dolls with Polymer Clay*, *The Polymer Clay Techniques Book* and *Creative Home Decor in Polymer Clay*. Sue has also written two major books on candle making as well as dozens of polymer clay articles for British and American magazines. Several more books are in the pipeline.

In 1997, with the enthusiastic help of several others, she founded the British Polymer Clay Guild. She manages to combine her writing with an active role in the guild, as well as teaching polymer clay classes all over the world.

Sue has many other interests. She plays the violin in a local orchestra, directs shows for a drama group, and spends every available moment of the summer sailing around the coasts of Britain and Europe. She is a qualified Yachtmaster Offshore. She has had two children's musicals published, which have been performed all over the world. She lives in a beautiful part of rural eastern England.

Polymer Clay Mosaics. Copyright © 2003 by Sue Heaser. Manufactured in China. All rights reserved. The patterns and drawings in the book are for personal use of the crafter. By permission of the author and publisher, they may be either hand-traced or photocopied to make single copies, but under no circumstances may they be resold or republished. It is permissible for the purchaser to make the projects contained herein and sell them at fairs, bazaars and craft shows. No other part of this book may be reproduced in any form or by any electronic or mechanical means including information storage and retrieval systems without permission in writing from the publisher, except by a reviewer, who may quote a brief passage in review. Published by North Light Books, an imprint of F&W Publications, Inc., 4700 East Galbraith Road, Cincinnati, Ohio 45236. (800) 289-0963. First edition.

07 06 05 04 03   5 4 3 2 1

Library of Congress Cataloging-in-Publication Data
Heaser, Sue.
   Polymer clay mosaics / by Sue Heaser.
      p. cm.
   Includes index.
   ISBN 1-58180-257-9 (alk. paper)
    1. Polymer clay craft. 2. Mosaics--Technique. I. Title.

TT297 .H433 2003
738.5--dc21
                        2002038926

Editors: Jane Friedman, Karen Roberts and Jolie Lamping Roth
Designer: Stephanie Strang
Layout Artist: Kathy Gardner
Production Coordinator: Michelle Ruberg
Photographers: Christine Polomsky, Al Parrish and Tim Grondin
Photo Stylist: Jan Nickum

metric conversion chart

TO CONVERT	TO	MULTIPLY BY
Inches	Centimeters	2.54
Centimeters	Inches	0.4
Feet	Centimeters	30.5
Centimeters	Feet	0.03
Yards	Meters	0.9
Meters	Yards	1.1
Sq. Inches	Sq. Centimeters	6.45
Sq. Centimeters	Sq. Inches	0.16
Sq. Feet	Sq. Meters	0.09
Sq. Meters	Sq. Feet	10.8
Sq. Yards	Sq. Meters	0.8
Sq. Meters	Sq. Yards	1.2
Pounds	Kilograms	0.45
Kilograms	Pounds	2.2
Ounces	Grams	28.4
Grams	Ounces	0.04

DEDICATION »

To Kathy and Tamsin–

who saved me from drowning and helped me

to listen to the skylark.

acknowledgments

I would like to thank my family and friends for their support and encouragement during the tempestuous times that coincided with the writing of this book. I would also like to thank my publisher, F&W, for their understanding and patience.

Thanks also to Polyform Products of Chicago, who supplied their wonderful clays to be used for the step-by-step photography.

TABLE OF

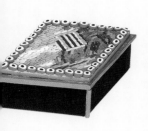

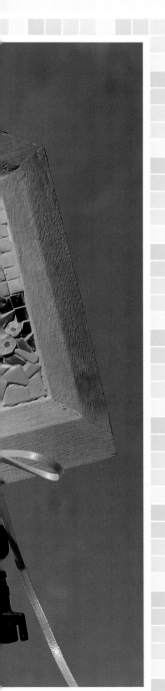

Classical Mosaics 22

Micromosaics 68

Pietre Dure Mosaics 86

Tile Mosaics 108

contents

Mosaics have fascinated me for as long as I can remember. When I was a child, my family traveled a good deal, and the first mosaic that I ever saw was on a ruined temple in the middle of an Asian desert. The temple walls were shedding tiny pieces of vivid turquoise tile into the sand, and I could just make out the glorious patterns that the pieces had fallen from. I was enchanted

intro duction

at such riches in a bleak landscape. When I grew up, the fascination continued, and my work in archaeology gave me the opportunity to study this lovely ancient art form in detail.

But why use polymer clay to make mosaics? The answer is simple: Polymer clay is one of the most exciting new art materials to have appeared in recent years, and it is perfect for making mosaics. Traditionally, mosaics are made with pieces of stone and ceramic, set into mortar or cement, but many people find these materials tough to work with: They are hard on your hands, and you need to be relatively strong to use them. Polymer clay, in contrast, is delightfully easy to work with, and PVA glues replace the harsh mortar and cement.

Polymer clay requires no special equipment; it is nontoxic and widely available; it comes in a huge range of colors and, when baked in an ordinary home oven, forms a permanent material that is colorfast and stable. Add to this the fact that polymer clay can simulate all kinds of stone, ceramic, glass and shell, and you have a dream material for making mosaics!

This book gives you all the information that you need to make a wonderful collection of mosaics with polymer clay. Whether you are a complete beginner or a seasoned polymer clay artist, you will find that the techniques given here are quick and easy to follow. Projects for traditional classical mosaics are given first, but there are many other exciting mosaic types, and the remaining chapters explore micromosaics, pietre dure and tile mosaics. Many designs are inspired by the ancient mosaics that I have discovered on my world travels, but pleasing modern designs are included, as well. I hope that you will enjoy these exciting projects and discover for yourself the satisfaction and delight of making mosaics.

materials

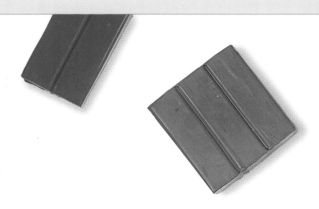

This chapter lists the materials you will need to make the projects in this book. These materials are normally easily obtainable—even in a tiny town like my own! If you have difficulty in finding any items, refer to the list of mail-order suppliers on page 125.

▶▶ polymer clay

Polymer clay is one of the most exciting new art materials to have been developed in recent times. Originally invented in the 1930s, it has now become a recognized art medium used by artists all over the world. Its extraordinary diversity of application means that it is used by a vast range of artists and craftsmen in many different genres from jewelry and sculpture to animation, fine art, home décor and doll making.

Polymer clay requires no special equipment or long apprenticeship—all you need to get started are a few blocks of clay, your hands and a home oven to harden the finished pieces. This means that the clays are very beginner-friendly, and they are accessible to home crafters everywhere. However, they also have enormous appeal to skilled professional artists who are continuously pushing the boundaries of the medium into new and exciting directions.

Polymer clay is a PVC or plastic modeling material that is hardened by baking at a relatively low temperature in a home oven. It is known by various brand names such as Fimo, Sculpey, Premo! Sculpey, Cernit and Creall-therm. The clay is made of fine particles of plastic combined with pigment and suspended in a liquid called a plasticizer. When the clay is baked, the particles of plastic fuse together to make a permanent solid plastic that is stable and colorfast and will last indefinitely. Baked clay is normally slightly flexible, although its strength will vary between brands.

Polymer clay has a very fine texture and is therefore ideal for detailed modeling techniques. The soft clay is easily shaped with fingers and simple tools; it can be formed into logs and balls, rolled into sheets, modeled, sculpted, extruded, textured, stamped and generally thoroughly enjoyed! Texture and malleability varies between brands but all the main brands of polymer clay can be used successfully to make mosaics.

Polymer clay comes in a wide range of colors that vary between brands and these can be mixed to make more colors, in the same way as artists' paints. This produces a huge palette of colors for making into mosaics. See page 16 for instructions on color mixing.

I like to use all the brands of clay for mosaics, often combining different brands in one mosaic, because this gives me such a wonderful range of colors. You can mix clays from different brands to get further colors, although I keep this to a minimum because there has been the occasional report of these clay mixtures not being very durable.

▶▶ clay texture

There is a considerable variation in texture between the brands of clay. Some clays are very soft, while others are hard and crumbly until they are kneaded. Sculpey III is one of the softest clays while Fimo Classic and Creall-therm are at the firmer end of the scale. Soft clays may become too soft for delicate work if you have hot hands. Firmer clays are not affected by body heat and are better for fine detail, although you will have to knead them thoroughly before use. See page 14 for how to adjust the texture of your clay.

▶▶ baked strength

Again, there is considerable variation between brands. Sculpey III is relatively weak after baking and Cernit is extremely strong with the other brands somewhere between the two. When making polymer clay mosaics that are glued onto a support, baked strength is not of prime importance. However, you should use one of the stronger clays for mosaics that are made into jewelry.

▸▸clay colors and types

Basic color range

All the main brands of polymer clay come in large color ranges that include primary and secondary colors, white, black and a variety of browns and grays depending on the brand. See page 16 for the list of colors used in the projects in this book. These basic colors are normally opaque and are all intermixable. Besides the basic colors, most major brands also contain the following colors and clay types: translucent, metallic and pearlescent, granite or stone effect, novelty, and liquid polymer clay.

Translucent clay

This is an extremely useful color and is sometimes called *Transparent* although this is a misnomer because there is no glass-clear polymer clay currently available. Translucent clay can be used to simulate quartz or marble when making mosaics and can be tinted with colored clay to make translucent pastels.

Metallic and pearlescent clays

These can really add sparkle to your work! There is considerable variation between the brands and some have large particles of glitter within the clay to provide the glitz while others contain mica powder to give an effect like satin.

Granite or stone effect clays

These clays, such as Sculpey Granitex and Fimo Stone Colors, have small particles of fibre or grit added to the body of the clay to give textured results that are excellent for simulating natural stone in mosaics. They come in a range of muted colors that can be used as they are or mixed together.

Novelty clays

These include fluorescent colors, glow-in-the-dark and flexible clays, and while they have more limited use in mosaics, they can provide accent and interest for imaginative projects.

Liquid polymer clay

This is a syrupy liquid that can be used for surface effects, glazes, faux enamel effects and many other exciting applications. It can also be used for grouting mosaics, but the mosaic needs to be baked after grouting to set the liquid clay. Tint liquid polymer clay with oil paints if required.

translucent

metallic and pearlescent

granite (stone effect)

▸▸storing polymer clay

Polymer clay has a shelf life of several years and, if it is stored carefully, will keep a long time. It does not dry out once the pack is opened, so there is rarely any wastage.

Keep your clay in a cool dark place, away from sunshine and any form of heat such as hot radiators. Heat is the worst enemy for polymer clay because, if excessive, it will partly bake the clay, which will then go hard and be unusable.

Once open, store the clay in sealed box or tin to keep it free from dust. If different colors are allowed to touch each other, they will be difficult to separate cleanly so either wrap them back in their packets or wrap in baking parchment. Sheets of mixed color or canes can be kept separate from each other by interleaving or wrapping in baking parchment.

Do not store unwrapped polymer clay in plastic boxes because the box may be damaged where the clay touches it.

▶▶ other materials

Apart from polymer clay, here are the other materials you will need to make polymer clay mosaics. The individual projects list the specific materials that are needed for that particular project.

Supports

These are the surfaces that you cover with mosaic. The projects use a wide variety of supports such as sheets of polymer clay, wooden boxes, thick cardboard, glassware and ceramic tiles. Polymer clay mosaic tiles can be glued to any clean, dry surface that is stable and unlikely to warp. The technique of applying mosaics used in this book does not require the clay to be baked on the support so this means that even wood and papier mâché can be used for the support.

Tracing paper

Tracing paper is used for transferring template designs to the support that is to be covered with the mosaic. You can also use transfer paper.

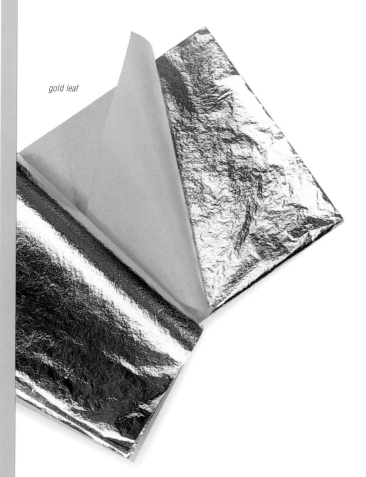

gold leaf

Graph paper

This is the secret weapon that makes cutting classical mosaic tiles, or tesserae, so easy! The graph paper is laid on the sheet of clay and pricked through with a needle to transfer a grid of cutting guidelines onto the clay below. For the projects I use imperial graph paper that is divided into ¼" squares, but you can use metric paper instead and prick every 6mm to make equal-size tesserae.

Talcum powder

You will need talcum powder to dust over the clay surface with a soft paintbrush to prevent sticking. If you are sensitive to talcum powder, use cornstarch (corn flour) instead.

Rubbing alcohol (methylated spirits)

This is useful for brushing over any surface that needs to be degreased before applying glue or paint. It is also good for cleaning polymer clay from your hands and work surface.

Artificial metal leaf

Polymer clay users have long enjoyed the effects of metal leaf on clay, and it can be used to make spectacular golden mosaics. Real gold leaf costs a fortune, but you can use the artificial kind instead, provided that you varnish the surface afterwards to prevent tarnishing (see page 11). Artificial leaf is available from arts and crafts stores.

Lazertran Silk

This proprietary paper allows you to make excellent photocopy transfers onto the polymer clay surface. The results are much clearer and more reliable than using ordinary paper. See pages 20-21 for more information on transferring images using photocopiers and page 125 for information on Lazertran Silk suppliers.

PVA glue

This is the best type of glue to use when gluing mosaic tiles to any kind of support. It is clean and easy to use and dries flexible and transparent. Craft tacky glues of various brands are the best.

▶▶ finishing materials

Once your mosaic is made, you will need a number of finishing materials to complete your project.

Grout

This is used for the classical mosaics and is worked over the finished mosaic to fill the gaps between the mosaic pieces and consolidate them. The color of the grout used for a particular mosaic is important because it draws the whole design together. It can be left white or tinted with acrylic paint to tone with the tiles.

I have tested many different kinds of grouting material over the years from softened polymer clay to household filler, liquid polymer clay to even glue and paint. I have found that the best of all is simply ordinary waterproof ceramic tile grout, of the kind used in bathrooms and kitchens. Ceramic tile grout usually comes in white or neutral colors and is available either ready-mixed, which is very easy to use, or in a powder form that has to have water added to it.

Acrylic paint

This is used to tint the grout to the required color. Add small quantities of paint first because it is much easier to add color than to lighten a cup of grout that you have made too dark!

Varnish

Polymer clay should be varnished only with compatible varnishes. Never use a solvent-based varnish on polymer clay because it will never dry. Several polymer clay manufacturers make their own varnish or you can use an acrylic varnish. It is only necessary to use varnish on polymer clay if you particularly want a shiny surface, or you have gold leaf or pearlescent powders to protect.

Rub 'n Buff

This is a proprietary metallic wax paste that is compatible with polymer clay. Rub 'n Buff can be rubbed or brushed onto the baked clay to gild it. Or you can use acrylic gold paint instead.

acrylic paint

Sandpaper

Polymer clay can be sanded very successfully and then buffed with stiff fabric to give a lovely sheen to its surface. Use wet/dry sandpaper, 400-, 600- or 800-grit. Wet/dry sandpaper is available from car body repair shops and home improvement or hardware stores.

Wax furniture polish

Finished classical mosaics sometimes have a cloudy surface from traces of grout. A quick rub with wax furniture polish will remove the film and give the mosaic a lovely soft shine.

Superglue (cyanoacrylate glue)

This type of glue is the best to use for gluing jewelry mosaics to metal findings, such as brooch backs and hair barrettes.

tools and equipment

Making mosaics with polymer clay requires only the simplest of tools and equipment, and you will probably find that you have most things already in your home. The tools and equipment given here are the basic things you will need for making the mosaics in this book; the individual projects list any specific items required for that project.

Ceramic tiles

I use ceramic tiles as my work surface for making mosaics, and it is a good idea to have several in different sizes, from small 6" (15cm) tiles to larger 8" (20cm) tiles. Plain white glazed tiles with no surface texture are the best. The tiles are a perfect surface for cutting out mosaic squares (tesserae) because the whole tile, clay and all, can then be placed directly in the oven for baking without disturbing and distorting the soft clay. They are also used in the same way for making micromosaics, pietre dure and tile mosaics.

Tissue blades

Long, sharp tissue blades have become vital tools for the polymer clay artist. They are widely available from polymer clay suppliers. Originally they were used for slicing millefiori canes, but they are also invaluable for making long straight cuts across a clay sheet to make mosaic tesserae, for cutting out tiles and for trimming straight edges.

Craft knife

A craft knife with a curved blade (as shown left) is useful for most polymer clay mosaics. It can be used as an appliqué tool and as a knife. However, a craft knife with a straight pointed blade is better for pietre dure mosaics.

tissue blade and craft knife

Pasta machine

A pasta machine is not an essential tool, but it does make working with polymer clay a lot more fun! A pasta machine is used to roll out sheets of clay of varying thickness, to condition clay, to mix clay colors and to create sheets of blended clay–all of which it does quickly and efficiently. Pasta machines sometimes produce streaks of black on the clay, which is caused by the aluminum of the rollers oxidizing between each use. Cleaning the machine helps only temporarily, so it is easier to simply roll a sheet of scrap clay through the machine a few times to clear the streaks when the problem occurs.

Roller

A roller is the manual alternative to a pasta machine, and you can use anything that is smooth, round and sturdy enough to roll out the clay. A transparent acrylic roller is best, because it does not stick to the clay and you can see through it as you roll, but a sturdy bottle, a piece of plastic pipe or a marble rolling pin will serve very well. I do not recommend using a printer's brayer, because you cannot apply enough pressure to roll out the clay smoothly when holding a handle. To roll out even sheets of a specific thickness, you will need to place strips of wood or cardboard on either side of the clay. Dollhouse stores sell wood strips in $^1/_{16}$" (1.5mm) and $^1/_8$" (3mm) thicknesses, and these are perfect.

Needles

You will need a pin or darning needle to prick out a grid through graph paper when making mosaic tesserae. A ball-headed pin is easy to hold. Large blunt wool or tapestry needles are used to scribe the clay before inlaying clay threads in pietre dure.

Cutters

Cutters for polymer clay are available in a wide range of shapes and sizes from polymer clay suppliers, craft stores and cooking equipment stores. The smaller sizes are particularly useful for instant inlay techniques (see the Taj Mahal Necklace project on page 90).

Grout spreader

You will need a spreader for applying grout. I like to use a small glue spreader, but a piece of stiff cardstock will do as well.

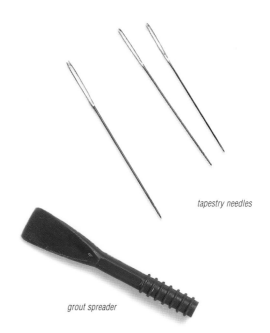

tapestry needles

grout spreader

safety!

All brands of polymer clay go through stringent safety checks before they are marketed. These checks also cover the baking and handling of the clays. All polymer clays are labeled nontoxic, and while they are not advised for food use, they are considerably safer to use than many well-known arts and crafts materials.

As with any craft material, take basic safety precautions when working with polymer clay:

▪ Wash your hands before and after using the clays.

▪ Do not use polymer clay tools and utensils for food, and do not allow either baked or unbaked polymer clay to come into contact with food.

▪ Do not allow the clays to burn. If this happens accidentally, you will know at once because the smell is disgusting, and you are unlikely to unwittingly breathe in any fumes because of this! Turn off the oven, open the windows and leave the room until the smell disperses.

▪ It is safe to use a domestic oven to bake your clay, but if you regularly bake in large quantities because you are selling your work, you may want to invest in a separate oven. This will avoid any buildup of plasticizer in your cooking oven and keep polymer clay smells away from the family dinner.

basic techniques

Please take the time to practice these basic techniques before you begin the projects. To avoid repetition in the project steps, all the main basic techniques are shown here, and you will find the projects much easier to follow if you have covered these first.

Most people usually find that they have learned basic polymer clay techniques as children when using modeling clay! Rolling balls and logs, shaping, pinching and squeezing all come naturally to tiny hands, and if you are a beginner with polymer clay, you will find that you can do most of these actions instinctively.

▶▶ preparing the clay

Polymer clay needs a certain amount of preparation before use, often called kneading or conditioning.

Conditioning by hand

To condition the clay by hand, open the packet of clay and cut off about one-quarter of the block. Roll this between your hands as though you were making a log (see page 15). When the clay starts to elongate, fold the log in half and roll again, repeating until the clay is soft enough so that when you bend the log into a U-bend, it does not crack. Cut off some more clay and repeat, combining with the first piece and so on. Firmer clays will need more conditioning than softer ones. You don't need to condition the clay for any longer than it takes to make it usable and malleable. Strength is not increased by lengthy conditioning, and some clays may become weaker if you continue too long, because air bubbles are incorporated into the clay.

Conditioning with a pasta machine

A pasta machine makes conditioning a delight–particularly when using softer clays that do not crumble.

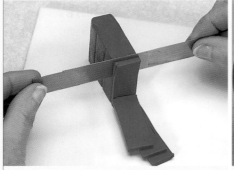

1 Use a tissue blade to cut slices, about ⅛" (3mm) thick, from the side of the clay block.

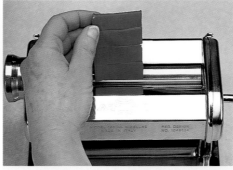

2 Set your pasta machine to the thickest setting. Press the clay slices together, side by side, and feed them into the pasta machine. Crank the handle, and the slices will be rolled into a sheet.

3 Fold the sheet in half and, placing the fold at the side so as to avoid air bubbles, pass the clay through the pasta machine again. Repeat five to six times, and the clay will be fully conditioned. Firm or crumbly clay will need more rollings.

Adjusting the clay texture

Different brands of clay vary considerably in texture between very soft and malleable to extremely firm. Texture may also vary within one brand of clay because it is affected by the different pigments used. It is possible to alter the texture of the clay considerably, and this is important for some projects.

Softening firm clay If your clay is very stiff and you find that it is crumbling when you try to roll it between your hands, it may be old stock. If it is painfully hard to work, take it back to the shop and exchange it! If it is stiff but workable, you can soften it by adding a proprietary softener. Sculpey Clay Softener (formerly Sculpey Diluent) is a liquid softener; only a few drops should be added to the clay while it is being conditioned. This softener can be used with any brand of clay. Or you can try Fimo Mix Quick, a soft form of clay. Simply knead into firm clay in the proportion of one part Mix Quick to at least two parts clay.

making clay sheets

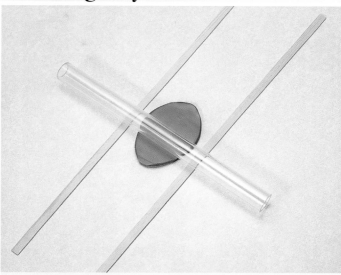

Leaching soft clay When is clay too soft? For mosaic making, firm clay is better to work with. If your clay distorts badly when you cut it, it is probably too soft for mosaics. In this case, the answer is leaching. Roll the clay out in thin sheets and sandwich these between sheets of white paper, pressing the paper firmly onto the clay. Leave for several hours and then peel off the paper. An oily mark will have appeared where the clay was in contact with the paper; this is the liquid plasticizer leaching out of the clay. Test the clay to see if it is firm enough, and if not, repeat with fresh paper. This technique is particularly useful for making pietre dure, which needs dry, firm clay for a successful result.

You will need to make polymer clay sheets repeatedly for the projects in this book. A pasta machine will do this for you and, if you enjoy working with polymer clay, is well worth the investment because it will also condition the clay rapidly (see page 14). However, it is not an essential piece of equipment, and an acrylic roller, as pictured above, or a sturdy glass bottle or piece of plastic pipe will do as well. Lay two thin strips of wood or cardboard of the thickness required on either side of the clay while you roll to ensure that the sheet is of uniform thickness.

making logs

Logs are one of the basic clay shapes that you will use repeatedly, and it is worth practicing how to make them smooth and even in thickness.

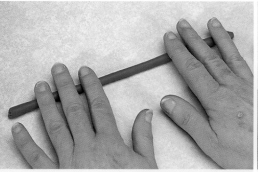

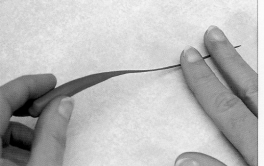

1 Shape the conditioned clay to make a rough log. Lay this between your palms and roll it back and forth, applying pressure to start making the log.

2 Lay the log on your work surface and roll it back and forth with your hands, applying light pressure and moving your fingers constantly up and down the length of the log to prevent any grooves forming. Continue until the log is of the thickness required.

3 To make fine threads of clay, hold the log in one hand and continue rolling the other end with your other hand. Keep moving your fingers up and down the length of the log as before, drawing the end out thinner and thinner. Holding the thicker part of the log in your nonworking hand gives you control over the thin clay thread and prevents hand heat from distorting it.

▶▶ clay colors

The polymer clay manufacturers all use different color names for their clays. Not all brands of clay are available to everyone, so this can be confusing if you are trying to substitute a particular color in one brand of clay for the equivalent color in another. One person's terra-cotta is another's dark brown! To avoid this problem, I have used descriptive names instead of brand names for the clay colors used in the projects in this book. The photograph shows these clay colors with their descriptive names so that you can match the color in the brand that you are using.

▶▶ mixtures

Some projects require mixtures of colors, and these are given as parts of a 2-ounce (or 65g) block of clay. Most clay blocks are easily divisible into quarters and sixteenths using the markings on the back of the block as guidance.

Smaller quantities for mixing are either given as balls of a particular size or as a trace, which is a very tiny amount that is too small to specify and will vary with different brands. In this case, mix in a tiny pinch of clay at a time until it matches the color in the photographs.

To mix the colors, roll them together into a log, fold the log in half and roll again. Repeat until all the streakiness has blended into the new color. If you have a pasta machine, roll the two colors out together, fold and roll again, repeating until the colors are completely blended.

▶▶ marbling

This is a useful technique with polymer clay and is the result of mixing colors only until they are streaky. The technique is covered in detail on page 89.

Basic clay colors

translucent	*white*	*black*	*yellow*	*golden yellow*	*orange*
red	*crimson*	*purple*	*navy blue*	*blue*	*turquoise*
blue-green	*green*	*leaf green*	*dark brown*	*beige*	*gray*

Specialty clays

granite	*gold*	*copper*	*pearl*

skinner blend

This wonderful technique, invented by Judith Skinner of the United States, is used to make sheets of graded clay colors.

Two-Color Skinner blend

1 Roll out two sheets of clay, one each of the two colors required, and both of the same thickness. Cut a right-angled triangle of the same size from each sheet. Assemble the triangles, with one flipped, to make a two-color rectangle and press along the diagonal to join the pieces together. Trim along the top and bottom of the rectangle so that the diagonal becomes offset.

2 With the sheet oriented in the same way as in the photograph, fold the sheet in half toward you. It is important to get this step right or you will not get a blend! The offset diagonal will ensure that a strip of unblended color runs down each side of the sheet after blending.

3 Pass the folded sheet, fold downward, through a medium setting on the pasta machine (or roll it flat with your roller).

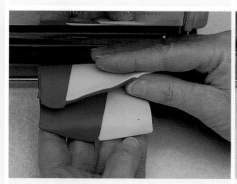

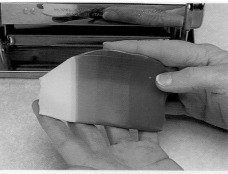

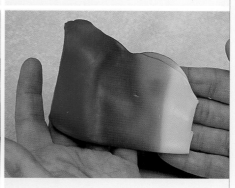

4 Always keeping the sheet oriented in the same way, fold in half again and pass through the pasta machine again. Repeat this process another ten times. Take care to always put the folded sheet into the pasta machine with the fold downward to minimize trapped air bubbles.

5 After about ten passes, the sheet shows how the colors blend to create a band of green in the center, with a yellow strip on one side and a blue strip on the other. Continue folding and passing through the pasta machine about twenty more times.

6 The sheet is fully blended when all streaks have disappeared and the colors grade smoothly into each other.

Multiple Skinner blend

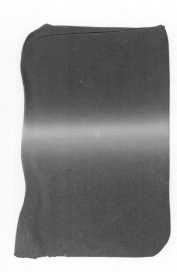

If three different-colored triangles are laid together as shown in the photograph, a three-part Skinner blend is produced. The triangle tips should be cut off as before to give a strip of the original color both at the sides as well as in the center, as in the case of the yellow in this example. The sheet is folded and rolled in the same way. You can make four- or even five-part blends using the same technique.

▶▶ strip blends

This technique produces blends that grade from one color to the other more rapidly. They are useful for mixing colors for micromosaics and pietre dure, which require sharp gradients between colors.

The steps given here show a two-color strip blend, but you can use three, four, or even five logs of color to make a multiple strip blend.

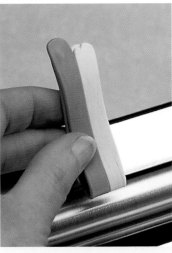

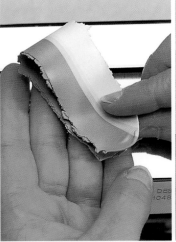

1 Form two logs of color, each about ¼" (6mm) thick and 3" (8cm) long. Squeeze them together and pass them lengthwise through the pasta machine.

2 Fold the strip in half, aligning the colors carefully, and pass through the pasta machine again, placing the fold into the machine first.

3 Continue folding the strip in half, aligning the colors carefully, and passing through the pasta machine until the two colors begin to blend in the middle of the strip. It is the inevitable slight inaccuracy in alignment when folding that gives the central blend.

4 After about twenty to thirty passes, the blend should be a smooth but steep gradient between the two colors and can now be used as required.

▶ millefiori caning

This is a favorite technique for polymer clay and gives many exciting effects. The name (literally "one thousand flowers") comes from the glassmaking technique that produces rods or canes of glass that have a pattern running all through the length like holiday candy or seaside rock. Slices cut from the canes are identically patterned and can be used in various decorative ways. The polymer clay version is relatively simple to master, and the basics are shown below.

Slicing millefiori canes

Once your cane is made and reduced, set it aside for a while to cool and become firmer before slicing. This will prevent the blade from squashing the cane as you slice. In hot weather, place the cane in a refrigerator for about 15 minutes. Using a very sharp tissue blade or craft knife, cut the cane into slices as thin as you can manage without distorting them. This is easiest to do if you look down on the cane and rotate it a quarter turn between each slice so as to minimize distortion.

Canes can be wrapped in baking parchment and stored for future use. Canes that have been stored will need warming in your hands before use.

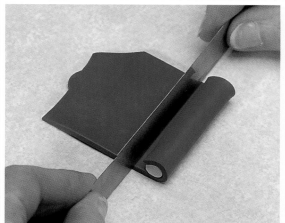

1 The simplest canes to make are bull's-eye canes: logs of one color wrapped in a sheet of another color. Form a ⅜" (10mm) thick log of white clay, about 2" (5cm) long. Roll out a ⅛" (3mm) thick sheet of blue clay and trim it to 2" (5cm) wide. Lay the white log on the blue sheet and roll it up until the first edge of the sheet meets the sheet again and makes a light impression. Unroll slightly to reveal the faint line, then cut along this line with your blade so that the sheet will fit exactly and the edges can be butted together. Roll the cane lightly on your work surface to consolidate it.

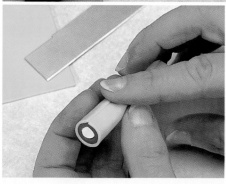

2 You can now wrap the cane with another sheet of different-colored clay for a more interesting cane. Here, a 1/16" (1.5mm) thick sheet of yellow clay is wrapped around the cane and the edges butted together as before.

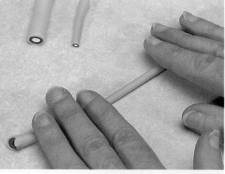

3 Once the cane is made, you can make it smaller in diameter so that the design inside is reduced, so that it looks amazingly detailed. This is called reducing the cane. To reduce a round section cane such as this, simply roll the cane on your work surface in the same way as making a log (see page 15) until it lengthens and thins. You can then cut slices of the cane with a tissue blade to use in mosaics.

4 More complex canes can be made by pressing together lengths of simple cane. Here, five bull's-eye canes of yellow clay wrapped in white have been pressed around an orange log to make a flower cane. An irregular shape such as this cannot be reduced by rolling or the petal shape will be lost. Instead, squeeze and pull the clay gently to lengthen it and reduce the diameter, working up and down the length of the cane and taking care not to break it.

▶▶ appliqué technique

The appliqué technique is invaluable for creating wonderful detail in polymer clay. It is used throughout the micromosaics chapter but is useful in many other kinds of polymer clay projects as well. It is rather like embroidering with clay, and once mastered, you will find that you can produce beautifully ornate work that would never be possible if you used your fingers.

A knife with a curved blade, like the one shown in the photographs, is an essential tool for this technique. A straight-bladed knife requires you to hold your hand too low and is almost impossible to use successfully for appliqué. Use firm or well-leached clay for this technique–it is difficult to achieve neat results with soft clay.

The demonstration below is taken from the Greek Temple Snuffbox project (pages 78-85).

1 Roll out a sheet of clay of the color required to ⅟₁₆" (1.5mm) thick. Cut a strip of clay of the width required in the project. To make square pieces, cut the strip the same width as the thickness of the clay sheet; for rectangular pieces, cut the strip wider. Lay this strip on the tile beside your working hand, angled so that you can cut slices easily. Cut a thin slice from the end of the strip with your knife and scoop it onto the knife tip as you cut.

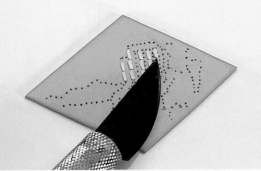

2 Turn the knife over and press the slice onto the clay background, positioning it accurately on the marked design. It will stick to the background as you press, and you will be able to remove the knife, leaving the tiny mosaic piece in place. Repeat for the next piece and continue, applying slices of color as required. It is important to pick up the clay slice at the very tip of the knife blade so that you can position it accurately when you turn the knife over and can no longer see the slice. If you know that it is at the very tip, you will know exactly where to press the knife down onto the clay background.

▶▶ transferring images

This is an exciting technique that is invaluable for transferring images onto the surface of polymer clay. It is used particularly for making polymer clay tiles that require repeating patterns but can be used in many other ways as well. Two methods are given here–the first uses ordinary photocopies and the second a special paper designed for making transfers.

Photocopy transfer

Photocopy transfer requires no special equipment apart from access to an ordinary toner-base photocopy machine or a laser printer. It can sometimes be a little hit-and-miss, because copiers and printers vary a lot. Try a test run first to make sure that the copier or printer that you are using will transfer onto polymer clay.

▶▶ **1. Photocopy the template** using an ordinary photocopy machine that has toner. Fresh photocopies work best. You can also scan the template and print with a laser printer that uses toner (an ink-jet printer will not work for this technique). You can color the image with colored pencils at this point.

▶▶ **2. Roll out the clay** and apply the copied image facedown onto a clay sheet. Rub the back of the paper firmly to ensure that the whole image is in contact with the clay.

▶▶ **3. Bake the clay** as usual and then peel back the paper to reveal the transferred image.

Lazertran Silk

This product is a type of paper that makes polymer clay transfer completely reliable. You can transfer color copies, as well. Do not use colored pencils on Lazertran paper. If you want the image in color, color the black-and-white image before copying it using a color copier.

▸▸ **1. Copy the image** onto the Lazertran Silk paper using a laser printer or a photocopier.

▸▸ **2. Apply the image** facedown onto the clay sheet and rub down well. Leave the image on the clay for 30 minutes.

▸▸ **3. Place the clay**, with the image still in place, into a bowl of water. This is easy to do if you are working on a ceramic tile. Simply immerse the whole tile, with the clay on it, in the water. After a few minutes, the paper will float away from the clay, leaving the image on the clay surface.

▸▸ **4. Remove the clay** from the water and allow it to dry naturally before baking in the usual way. After baking, the image on the clay will be dark, clear and permanent.

▸▸ adding soft clay to baked clay

Polymer clay can be baked many times without harm. This is useful if you want to bake a project before it is finished and then add more clay later and bake again. Smear some PVA glue onto the baked clay and allow it to dry. The PVA glue will provide an adhesive surface on the baked clay so that the fresh clay sticks firmly to it. After baking, the glue will form a strong bond.

▸▸ baking

Polymer clay should be baked in an ordinary domestic oven as recommended on the package. Most polymer clays should be baked at 275°F (135°C) for about 20 to 30 minutes per ¼" (6mm) thickness. After baking, most clays are slightly flexible and become harder as they cool.

It is important to bake polymer clay properly. Underbaked clay will be fragile, while overbaked clay will discolor. If allowed to actually burn, clay can give off toxic fumes. Baking longer than 30 minutes will not harm the clay, and it can be baked repeatedly; you can add fresh clay to a baked piece and rebake as necessary.

The critical factor is the temperature of the oven. If you have not used polymer clay before, it is wise to bake some test pieces to check that your oven is baking at the stated temperature. If the clay is very fragile after baking and crumbles if you try to break it, your oven is not hot enough. If the clay is discolored or shiny, the oven is too hot. Adjust the oven by 10° and test again. (This test works for most brands apart from Sculpey III, which is brittle and always relatively fragile after baking.)

Polymer clay should be baked on a ceramic tile, or on a cookie sheet that has first been covered with a piece of cardstock or baking parchment. Do not bake on bare metal, or the clay may scorch where it touches the metal. If you do not want the smell of clay pervading your oven, bake the clay in a deep ovenproof dish covered with a lid of aluminum foil (see page 13 for safety while baking).

▸▸ sanding

Baked polymer clay can be successfully sanded to smooth the surface or adjust imperfections in the clay. Use wet/dry sandpaper in 400-, 600- or 800-grit, which is available from home supply stores. Hold the clay under gently running water and sand. If the piece needs a lot of smoothing, start with a coarser grit and then continue with a finer grit. After sanding, buff the surface of the clay with a piece of stiff fabric or quilt batting. If you have a hobby drill, a buffing attachment will produce an excellent shine.

▸▸ cleaning up

Polymer clay is not a messy material, but you may find that your hands become sticky after a lot of handling. Clean your hands with baby wipes or a cloth and rubbing alcohol (methylated spirits) and then wash with soap and water. Keep your work surface clean by wiping it with a baby wipe or alcohol to remove dust or lint flecks that can spoil light-colored clays. It is also wise to clean your hands between clay colors for the same reason.

Mosaics are found in cultures all over the world, from decorated temples in the Far East to Roman villas in Europe and masks and jewelry in South America. The mosaics in this section are based on the type of mosaic developed by the Romans between 100 B.C. and A.D. 400. These were mostly used as decoration for the fabulous villas of the period and many beautiful examples are still in

classical mosaics

existence all over Europe today. The technique was continued into the Byzantine era to embellish the interiors of churches across Europe and the Middle East. Naturally colored stone was cut into little squares called "tesserae," which were pressed into a bed of mortar to make patterns and images. The color palette was enlarged with the use of ceramic tiles, pottery, glass and mother-of-pearl, all of which were cut to make tesserae, as well.

Making classical-style mosaics with polymer clay is much easier than using the Roman technique! You don't need to cut hard stone or ceramic tile to make your tesserae or mosaic tiles; the squares are cut from soft sheets of clay, so you can make the tiles quickly and easily. These are then baked and glued into the designs with PVA glue, which is far easier to use and more convenient than the traditional mortar. Polymer clay comes in many wonderful colors and textures, so you can simulate virtually every type of stone to replicate ancient mosaics, or you can go really wild and use a truly modern palette. The choice is yours!

Polymer clay mosaics are much lighter than traditional stone or ceramic mosaics, so they are ideal for decorating all kinds of artifacts, such as boxes, tiles, wall panels, trivets, furniture and other home décor items. However, polymer clay is not durable in frost or UV (ultraviolet) light, so it should not be used out-of-doors for garden mosaics. ■

basic techniques

I have tried many different ways of making classical mosaics with polymer clay, and the following techniques are the ones that I find quickest and easiest—and also great fun to do!

▸▸ making mosaic tiles

This is an easy technique to make lots of tesserae, or mosaic tiles, very quickly.

▸▸ Always roll out your clay to the same thickness. If you use a pasta machine to roll out the sheets, a medium setting such as 4, or ¹/₁₆" (1.5mm), is the best. If you use a roller and wood strips (see page 15), always use the same wood strips!

▸▸ Using a thickness of ¹/₁₆" (1.5mm) for your clay sheets, a half block of clay (1 ounce or 32g) will make a sheet measuring about 5" x 3½" (13cm x 9cm).

▸▸ It is always useful to make more mosaic tiles of each color than you need at the time: Store them by their individual colors in bags or jars to use in a future project.

materials

- 2-ounce (or 65g) blocks of polymer clay: ½ block in the color required
- ceramic baking tile
- graph paper
- pin (or needle)
- tissue blade

1 MAKE THE CLAY SHEET
Roll the clay into a sheet ¹/₁₆" (1.5mm) thick. Lay this onto a ceramic baking tile and smooth away any air bubbles trapped under the sheet. Lay the graph paper on the clay, pressing it down lightly.

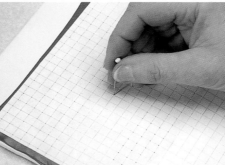

2 PRICK THE GRID
Use the pin to prick over the sheet, making a prick at the corner of each ¼" (6mm) square of the graph paper. This will impress a grid onto the clay below. After you have pricked over the graph paper once, you can use this same sheet over and over again: Simply lay it onto a sheet of clay and rub it down firmly, and the pinholes will impress a grid onto the clay.

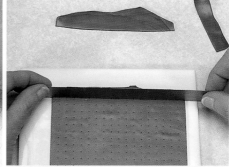

3 TRIM THE SHEET
Remove the graph paper and use the tissue blade to cut along the outer lines of the impressed grid to trim the clay sheet into a rectangle. Remove the scrap clay from around the sheet. Take care not to disturb the sheet of clay; it will not be removed from the tile until after baking.

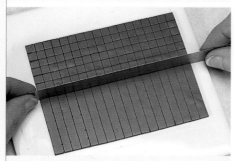

4 CUT THE MOSAIC TILES
Use the grid as a guide to cut along the lines of pricked holes. As you make each cut, rock the blade to and fro to open the cut slightly. With clays that are sticky in texture, this prevents the tiles from being disturbed as you remove the blade.

5 BAKE AND FINISH
Bake the cut sheet on the ceramic tile for 20 minutes. Allow the clay to cool on the tile and then remove the sheet from the tile by slicing under it with your blade. You will then find that you can break the mosaic tiles apart easily by bending them backwards along the lines of the cuts.

►► assembling the mosaics

Once the mosaic tiles are made, you are ready to trace your design and make the mosaic. The techniques of making a mosaic will vary a lot depending on the pattern, and this is covered in full under each project.

Grouting

After the mosaic tiles have been glued into place, the mosaic will need to be grouted. This will consolidate and fix the mosaic tiles and fill in any large gaps between them.

Before grouting, always leave a mosaic for several hours to allow the glue and any varnish (if used) to dry thoroughly.

Always read the instructions on the grout you are using; drying times can vary.

materials

- ready-mixed tile grout
- shallow dish
- acrylic paint in the color(s) required
- grout spreader (or piece of stiff cardstock)
- soft cloth
- bowl of warm water
- wax furniture polish

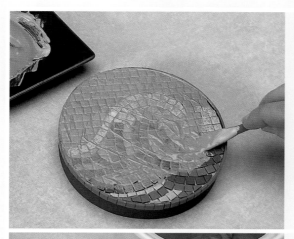

1 PREPARE AND SPREAD THE GROUT

Spoon the grout into the dish. You will need about one dessert spoon of grout for a mosaic 4" (10cm) square, depending on how tightly set the tiles are. Stir in a small amount of acrylic paint of the color required. Start with a small amount and then add more paint if necessary. Mix thoroughly and then apply the grout to the mosaic with a spreader or piece of stiff cardstock, pressing it into the spaces between the tiles. For a large mosaic, work over a section at a time.

2 CLEAN THE MOSAIC SURFACE

Wipe away the excess grout with a damp cloth. You will need to rinse the cloth and squeeze it almost dry, then wipe again several times. Try to get as much grout off the surface of the mosaic as possible.

4 POLISH THE MOSAIC

Leave the grout to dry for about 30 minutes and then buff away any grout remaining on the surface with a soft dry cloth. Leave to dry overnight and then polish lightly with wax furniture polish to give the clay's surface a lovely sheen.

3 REAPPLY THE GROUT IF NECESSARY

After wiping away the excess grout, you may find small areas that need a reapplication.

topiary tiles

These little tiles make a perfect beginners' project and would look delightful fixed to a kitchen or bathroom wall. Alternatively, you can glue a square of felt to the back of each tile to make unusual coasters. The design is based on nineteenth-century sampler motifs. Tapestry and cross-stitch designs work well for mosaics because they are based on a grid. ■

Trees were popular motifs in antiquity. This detail from my sketchbook shows a Byzantine mosaic from Jordan

materials

- 2-ounce (or 65g) blocks of polymer clay: ½ block of beige *(Premo! Ecru)*, ¼ block of copper, ¼ block of leaf green, ¼ block of navy blue, scraps of golden yellow
- pasta machine *(or roller and wood strips)*
- ceramic baking tile
- 4¼" (11cm) square ceramic tile
- graph paper, pricked
- tissue blade
- rubbing alcohol *(methylated spirits)*
- tracing paper and pencil
- PVA glue
- craft knife
- tile grout
- brown acrylic paint
- grout spreader
- soft cloth
- wax furniture polish

(the materials listed above are needed for each tile)

preparation

- **tiles:** Make ¼" (6mm) mosaic tiles from the clay quantities given in the materials list and bake (see page 24 for basic techniques). Make three mosaic tiles from the golden yellow and bake.

Project pattern

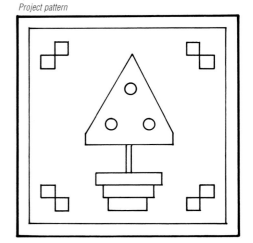

2nd tile pattern (see page 31)

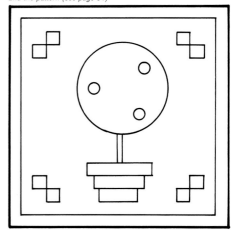

Enlarge patterns at 182% to bring to full size.

STEP 1: trace the design onto the tile

Wipe over the tile with alcohol to degrease the surface. Trace the template onto the tracing paper; flip over the paper and lay it onto the ceramic tile. Draw over the back of the design to transfer the pattern to the tile. Squeeze a line of glue along the bottom edge of the tile.

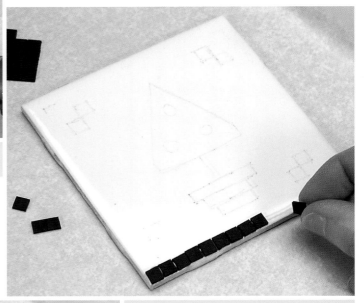

STEP 2: apply the border

Press a line of navy blue mosaic tiles along the line of glue, spacing them slightly apart and keeping them aligned with the outer edge.

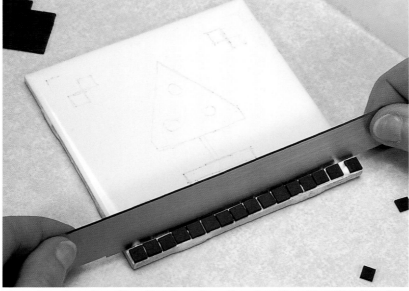

STEP 3: keep the lines straight

It is important to keep the lines of mosaic tiles as horizontal as possible, so while the glue is still wet, use a straightedge such as a tissue blade to push against the row of mosaic tiles to align them.

STEP 4: make the corners

When you reach the end of the row, if the mosaic tiles do not fit exactly, lay a whole tile at the corner and cut another tile to fit into the gap. Polymer clay tiles are easy to cut with a craft knife. Continue around the tile to make a single-row navy blue border.

STEP 5: begin the background and pot

Lay a line of beige tiles along the bottom border. Lay three copper tiles along the line of the pot's bottom, on top of this first beige line. Working upward, lay copper tiles in two more rows to complete the pot.

STEP 6: fill in the background

Fill in the background on either side of the pot with beige tiles, keeping the lines straight. Place two pairs of copper tiles where indicated in the design to embellish the corners.

STEP 7: begin the tree foliage

Apply glue to the foliage of the tree. Press a row of leaf green tiles along the bottom edge of the foliage. Use the tissue blade to ensure they are straight.

STEP 8: complete the foliage outline

Continue around the triangle of foliage, cutting tiles to fit as necessary. At the top of the tree, cut the tiles symmetrically to make a point.

STEP 9: make the golden apples

Trim the corners of each of the three golden yellow tiles to make them round. Glue them in place on the foliage.

STEP 10: add more foliage

Fill in the area between the apples with more leaf green tiles. Cut the tiles at an angle where they meet each other in the center of the tree. Cut a navy blue tile in half and apply the pieces in a line between the foliage and the pot for the trunk.

STEP 11: fill in gaps in the foliage

Cut small pieces of leaf green tile to fill in any large spaces around the apples. Tiny triangles will fit best.

STEP 12: lay in the upper background

Working upward, continue to lay lines of beige tiles, cutting them to fit against the tree and keeping them horizontal. Work from the edges toward the tree so that you need to cut only the tiles next to the tree. Apply pairs of copper tiles at the upper corners to match the lower corners.

STEP 13: grout the mosaic

Leave the glue to dry for a few hours. Mix brown acrylic paint into a tablespoon of grout to make a light brown color. Grout the mosaic, following the instructions on page 25. Leave the mosaic to dry overnight and then polish lightly with furniture polish.

▸▸**make a second tile:** The second tile is made in the same way, but with the leaf green tiles glued in a circle for the tree foliage and then filled in with leaf green and the three golden yellow apples.

wave box

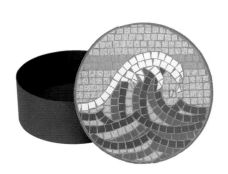

The design and lovely misty colors of this stylish box were inspired by Japanese prints and demonstrate how arranging mosaic tiles in loops and swirls can give a wonderful feeling of movement to an image. Polymer clay mosaics are much lighter than conventional mosaics that use glass and ceramic tiles, so they are perfect for decorating wood and papier mâché items. This project uses Sculpey Granitex, a textured clay, but you can substitute similar colors instead. ■

materials

- 2-ounce (or 65g) blocks of polymer clay: ½ block of black Granitex, ⅜ block of gray, ⅛ block of turquoise, ¼ block of turquoise Granitex, ¼ block of white, ⅛ block of violet Granitex *(see mixture below)*
- pasta machine *(or roller and wood strips)*
- ceramic baking tiles
- 4½" (12cm) diameter round wooden box
- graph paper, pricked
- tissue blade
- black, blue and white acrylic paint
- paintbrush
- tracing paper and pencil
- PVA glue
- craft knife
- tile grout
- grout spreader
- soft cloth
- wax furniture polish

mixture

- **blue-gray** = ⅛ block of turquoise + ⅛ block of gray

preparation

- **tile:** Make ¼" (6mm) mosaic tiles from the clay colors listed to the left and bake (see page 24 for basic techniques).

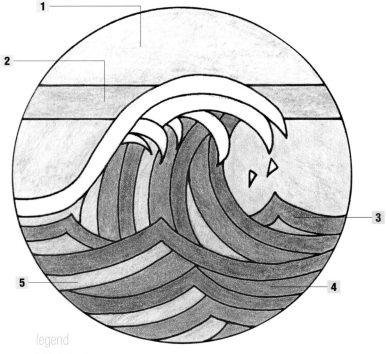

legend

1: black Granitex
2: violet Granitex
3: gray
4: blue-gray
5: turquoise Granitex

Enlarge pattern at 125% to bring to full size.

wave box

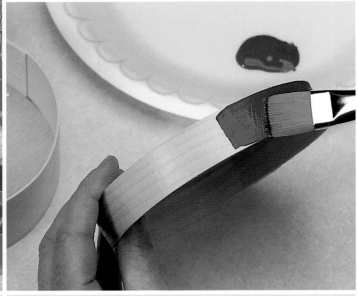

▶▶ STEP 1: **paint the box**

Mix a little black and blue paint into the white paint to make a blue-gray to match the color of the blue-gray clay. Paint the sides of the box evenly all over but leave the top of the lid unpainted so that the mosaic will be glued onto bare wood.

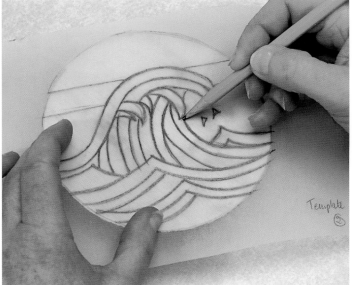

STEP 2: **trace the design onto the box lid**

Trace the template onto the tracing paper. Turn over the tracing paper and pencil along the lines on the back. Lay the tracing paper onto the box lid, centering the design, and trace over the lines to transfer the design to the lid.

STEP 3: **apply the white tesserae**

Spread a thin layer of PVA glue along the line marking the crest of the wave. Press on a line of white tiles. Cut the last two tiles at an angle so that the crest ends in a point.

STEP 4: create the wave curls

Lay another line of white tiles under the first line and then apply the four smaller lines in curls below this. The tiles at the end of each curl should be cut into a point to suggest the curling edge of the foam. Apply two small triangles of white below the crest to suggest spray.

STEP 5: apply the gray lines

Spread a thin line of glue along the lines of the large foreground wave and apply gray tiles along these lines.

STEP 6: cut the tiles   ▶▶

Cut the tiles at an angle where they meet the edge of the box lid. This is easiest to do by holding the tile to be cut in place and scratching the cutting line onto it with your craft knife. Then cut the tile along the mark.

STEP 7: add the vertical lines

Apply gray tiles to the upright lines of the main wave, cutting the tiles to fit neatly against the white foam and against the foreground waves.

STEP 8: apply the blue-gray tiles

Apply the blue-gray tiles in lines against the gray tiles on the main wave, cutting them to fit as necessary. Now apply the blue-gray tiles to the foreground waves. It is easier to apply glue to the back of the smaller pieces, then stick them in place.

STEP 9: apply the turquoise lines

Now apply turquoise Granitex tiles to the remaining spaces between the gray and blue-gray lines, cutting the tiles to fit as before.

STEP 10: make the lines of the cloud

Apply two lines of violet Granitex tiles along the line in the center of the sky, cutting them to fit where they butt against the curve of the wave crest and at the edges of the box.

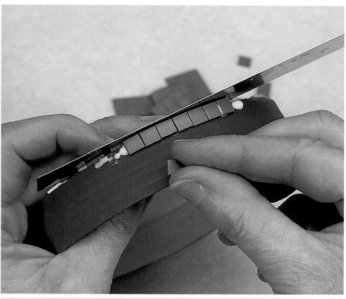

STEP 11: fill in the remaining sky

Now work upward with horizontal lines of black Granitex tiles toward the top of the box lid, cutting the tiles at the edges to fit the curve of the box. Finally work down from the lines of violet Granitex tiles, cutting the black Granitex tiles to fit against the wave. You will need to cut carefully to fit the background color around the white triangles of foam under the wave crest.

STEP 12: add the edge tesserae

Spread a line of glue around the upper outside edge of the box lid and apply blue-gray tiles all around. Take care that the top edge of each tile is flush with the top of the mosaic design. Use a tissue blade held on the top of the box as a guide.

STEP 13: finish by grouting

Leave the mosaic to dry. Mix a little black and blue acrylic paint into the grout to make a blue-gray to match the box. Follow the grouting instructions on page 25 to grout the mosaic.

translucent fall vase

Translucent clays are always exciting to work with. This project uses a combination of tinted translucent mosaic tiles on a glass vase. When the vase is displayed on a windowsill, the mosaic is lit from behind to give a splendid glow of autumn color. The vase could also be used as a candle lamp—either with a votive candle inside or partly filled with water and floating candles placed on the water's surface.

Translucent clay needs only very tiny quantities of colored clay to tint it, so take care when mixing. ■

materials

- 2-ounce (or 65g) blocks of polymer clay: 1 block of translucent; 1/16 block each of dark brown, gold, golden yellow, green, orange, purple (see mixtures below)
- pasta machine (or roller and wood strips)
- ceramic baking tiles
- rectangular glass vase, about 6" tall, 4" wide and 3" deep (15cm x 10cm x 8cm)
- graph paper, pricked
- tissue blade
- tracing paper and pencil
- tape
- rubbing alcohol (methylated spirits)
- PVA glue
- glass etching spray (glass frosting spray)

mixtures

- **golden brown** = 1/16 block of gold + 1/16 block of dark brown
- **translucent green** = 1/8 block of translucent + 1/4" (6mm) ball of green
- **translucent mauve** = 1/8 block of translucent + 1/4" (6mm) ball of purple
- **translucent orange** = 1/8 block of translucent + 1/4" (6mm) ball of orange
- **translucent yellow** = 1/8 block of translucent + 1/4" (6mm) ball of golden yellow
- **translucent yellow-green** = 1/8 block of translucent + 1/4" (6mm) ball of yellow and trace of green

The pattern appears here at full size.

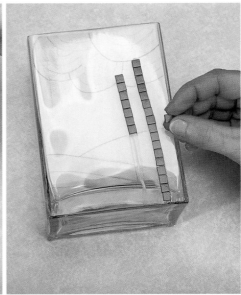

Mix the translucent colored clays as listed in the materials list. Quantities given are for guidance only, because color strength will depend on the clay brand. It is best to try mixing a small piece first to assess the proportions required. The baked tiles on the right of the photo above show how the color intensifies after baking. Roll out each color mixture into a sheet and follow the instructions on page 24 to make and bake the tiles.

STEP 2: **trace the design**

Trace the template onto tracing paper, adjusting the size, if necessary, to fit the side of your vase. Trim the template so that it will fit inside the vase, and tape it to the inside. Wipe over the surface of the glass with rubbing alcohol (methylated spirits) to degrease it.

STEP 3: **apply the tree trunks**

Spread PVA glue along the lines of the trunks. Press golden brown tiles in a line along each trunk, starting at the top and working down. Trim the two bottom tiles to fit flush with the base of the vase, if necessary.

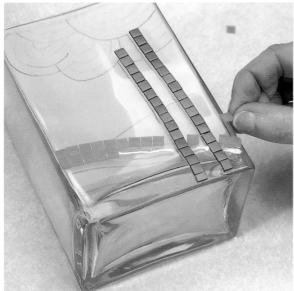

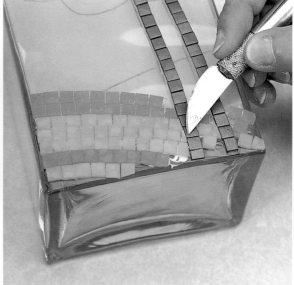

STEP 4: **begin the foreground hill**

Glue a row of translucent green tiles along the line of the top of the foreground hill, cutting the tiles to fit where they meet the trunks. Repeat to make a second row of translucent green below the first.

STEP 5:
complete the foreground hill

Working downward, lay three rows of translucent yellow-green tiles below the translucent green, following the curve of the first rows. Continue down, alternating rows of green with yellow-green.

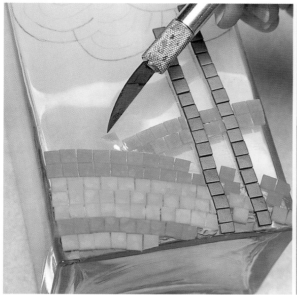

STEP 6: apply the distant hill

Glue a row of translucent mauve tiles along the line of the top of the distant hill, cutting the tiles to fit where they meet the trunks and the foreground hill. Work downward in rows of translucent mauve in the same way, following the curve and filling in the entire space.

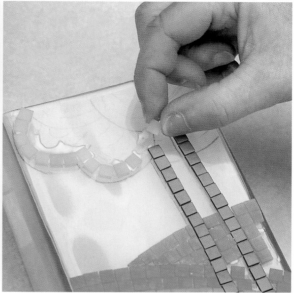

STEP 7: make the tree foliage

Apply glue to the foliage area of the tree. Glue translucent yellow and translucent yellow-green tiles in curves along the bottom line of the foliage, angling the tiles around the curves. Do not fit the tiles tightly together; a more spaced look gives the effect of dappled foliage.

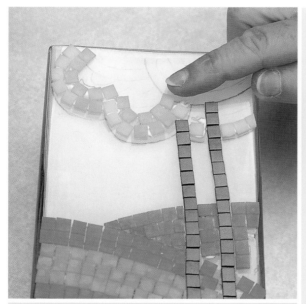

STEP 8:
fill in the remaining foliage

Apply curved rows of translucent orange tiles inside the first curves, and continue upward, following the curved lines and alternating the three colors randomly to give the effect of fall foliage.

STEP 9: spray with glass etching

When all the glue is dry, stand the vase on a sheet of paper and spray the whole design lightly with glass etching (glass frosting), following the instructions on the can. This will frost the sky area of the design, as well as any larger spaces between the tesserae. This mosaic is not grouted, so that the maximum amount of light will shine through the vase.

grapes tray

unches of grapes have been a popular motif for mosaics for centuries. This design is based on a Byzantine mosaic from Lebanon in the Middle East. The background uses a mosaic technique called "opus vermiculatum" where the lines of tesserae flow in curves around the design to produce a lovely fluid effect. ■

materials

- 2-ounce (or 65g) blocks of polymer clay: 1¼ blocks of white, ¼ block of gold, ¼ block of leaf green, ⅛ block of golden yellow ⅛ block of crimson, ⅛ block of navy blue, ⅛ block of purple, ⅛ block of violet Granitex, 1⁄16 block of dark brown, scraps of copper and golden yellow *(see mixtures below)*
- pasta machine *(or roller and wood strips)*
- ceramic baking tile
- hexagonal wooden tray *[or 11" (28cm) diameter round tray]*
- graph paper, pricked
- tissue blade
- gold paint *(or interior Brush 'n Leaf)*
- paintbrush
- tracing paper and pencil
- PVA glue
- tile grout
- black acrylic paint
- grout spreader
- soft cloth
- wax furniture polish
- matte varnish

mixtures

- **grape** = ⅛ block of purple + ⅛ block of crimson + ⅛ block of white
- **light leaf green** = ⅛ block of leaf green + ⅛ block of golden yellow *(marble lightly following the instructions on page 89)*

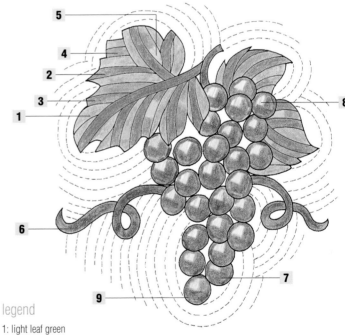

legend

1: light leaf green

2: leaf green

3: copper

4: gold

5: golden yellow

6: dark brown

7: grape

8: violet Granitex

9: navy blue

Enlarge pattern at 200% to bring to full size.

STEP 1: paint the edges

Follow the instructions on page 24 to make ¼" (6mm) tiles from the mixtures given on page 42 and from the remaining clay colors. Paint the edges of the tray gold, using gold paint or interior Brush 'n Leaf. Allow to dry.

STEP 2: trace the design onto the tray

Trace the template onto tracing paper. You may need to enlarge or reduce the design to fit your chosen tray. Turn over the tracing paper and pencil along the lines on the back. Lay the tracing paper onto the tray, positioning the design in the center, and trace over the lines again to transfer the design to the tray.

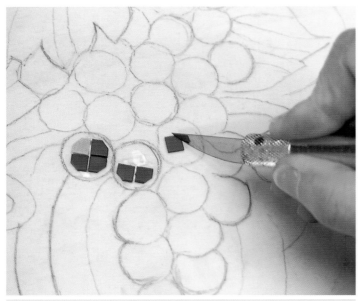

STEP 3: make the grapes

Spread a thin layer of PVA glue over some of the grapes. Cut one corner off each of three grape tiles and position them onto three sides of a grape outline so that the cut corners form the round shape. Cut one corner off a violet Granitex tile and lay this onto the top left corner of the grape for a highlight.

STEP 4: outline the grapes

Cut some navy blue tiles into three, lengthwise. Use these thin strips to outline the grape, trimming to fit as necessary. Repeat to apply tiles to all the remaining grapes. Where a grape is partly behind another, you will not need all the pieces.

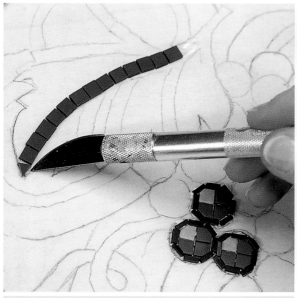

STEP 5: begin the leaves

Apply leaf green tiles along the center line and veins of the leaves, trimming each last tile at the leaf's edge into a point.

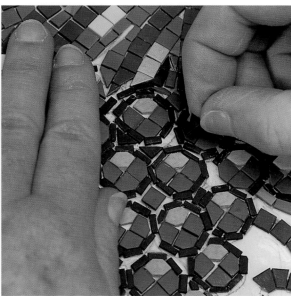

STEP 6: fill in the leaves

Fill in each leaf between the veins with light leaf green, golden yellow and copper tesserae, varying the colors to make a pleasing streaked effect. Again, cut the tiles at the edges of each leaf so they make a zigzag edge.

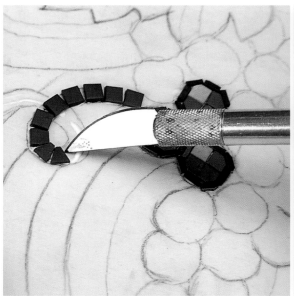

STEP 7: add the tendrils and stalk

Spread a line of glue along the tendrils and apply dark brown tiles in curved lines. Cut the tiles to fit as you go round the tendrils' loops, and cut the final tile into a point. Apply a line of dark brown tiles to make the stalk.

STEP 8: fill in the spaces

Fill in any large gaps among the grapes with grape tiles cut to fit.

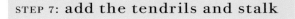

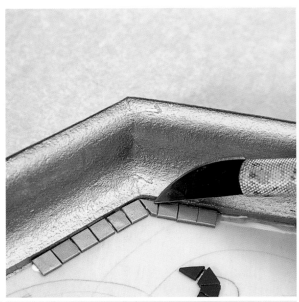

STEP 9: add the border

Apply glue and press gold tiles in a single line all around the edge of the tray. You will need to cut the corner tiles to fit if you are using a hexagonal tray as shown here.

STEP 10: start the background

Using the curved background lines as guides, and starting at the first line from the bunch of grapes, glue lines of white tiles along each line. You don't need to cut the tesserae; simply angle them as you go round each curve.

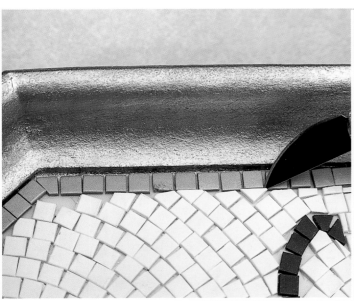

STEP 11: fill in the background

Now work outward, toward the edge of the tray, gluing tiles round each initial line and following the curve. When you reach the edges of the tray, you will need to trim the tiles to fit against the gold tiles.

STEP 12: fill in the background around the grapes

Work inward from the first line of background, cutting the tiles to fit neatly against the edges of the design. When the mosaic is finished, leave it to dry overnight.

STEP 13: **apply the grout**

Mix a little black paint into the grout to make a pale, neutral gray.
Follow the instructions on page 25 to grout the mosaic.

STEP 14: **clean the mosaic surface**

Wipe away the excess grout with a damp cloth. Leave the grout to dry for
about 30 minutes and then buff away any grout remaining on the surface.
Leave to dry overnight and then polish lightly with furniture polish.

STEP 15: **seal the surface**

Seal the surface of the mosaic with matte varnish to make the tray easier to clean.

byzantine sconce

his opulent mosaic depicts the jewel-encrusted walls of Jerusalem and is adapted from the superb sixth-century mosaics in the Basilica of St. Vitale in Ravenna, Italy. Artificial gold leaf is used to make the gleaming gold tesserae that shine in the candlelight when the sconce is lit. ■

materials

- 2-ounce (or 65g) blocks of polymer clay: 1 block of gold; ½ block of red pearl; ¼ block each of blue-green, blue pearl, copper, dark brown, navy blue, pearl; ⅛ block of gray; ⅛ block of turquoise *(see mixtures below)*
- pasta machine *(or roller and wood strips)*
- ceramic baking tiles
- 13" x 5½" (33cm x 14cm) wooden rectangle, ⅛" (3mm) thick
- 5½" x 3½" (14cm x 9cm) wooden rectangle, ½" (13mm) thick
- graph paper, pricked
- gold leaf *(transfer leaf is easier to use for this project but you can use ordinary loose leaf instead)*
- soft brush
- tissue blade
- gloss varnish
- talcum powder
- ¼" (6mm) circle cutter
- sandpaper
- hanging loop
- tacks and a hammer
- PVA glue
- tile grout
- black acrylic paint
- grout spreader
- wax furniture polish
- gold Rub 'n Buff *(or gold paint)*
- wood glue

mixtures

- **blue-gray** = ⅛ block of turquoise + ⅛ block of gray
- **golden brown** = 1/16 block of gold + 1/16 block of dark brown
- **pale blue-green** = ½" (13mm) ball of pearl + trace of blue-green

preparation

- **tile:** Set aside the pearl and red pearl clays. Make ¼" (6mm) mosaic tiles using the remaining clay colors and color mixtures given in the materials list and bake (see page 24 for basic techniques).

Enlarge pattern at 200% to bring to full size.

STEP 1: make the gold leaf mosaic tiles

Roll out a sheet of red pearl clay on a ceramic tile (red is a traditional undercoat for gold leaf and enriches its effect). Prick and cut the mosaic tiles as usual. Now lay a sheet of artificial gold leaf onto the clay. If you are using transfer leaf, you can use its backing sheet to help position it.

STEP 2: mark and bake the gold leaf tiles

Brush the surface of the gold leaf with a soft brush to smooth it onto the soft clay surface. Gently mark along the lines between the tiles with a tissue blade to cut the leaf neatly. Bake on the tile for 20 minutes.

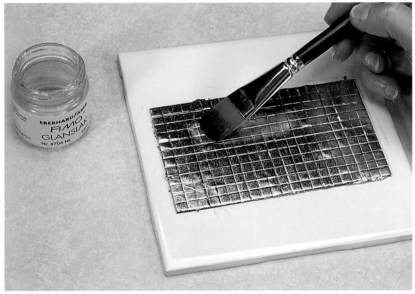

STEP 3: varnish the gold leaf tiles

When the tiles have cooled, varnish the surface with gloss varnish. This consolidates the leaf and protects it from tarnishing. When the varnish is dry, remove the sheet from the ceramic tile.

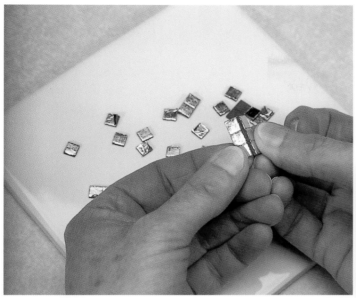

STEP 4: separate the tiles

Carefully snap the pieces apart by bending them backwards away from the leaf. Some of the leaf at the edges of the mosaic tiles may come off and reveal the red beneath, but this adds to the impression of age.

STEP 5: make the pearl rounds

Roll out the pearl clay into a sheet. Lay this on a ceramic tile, brush lightly with talcum powder to prevent sticking, and cut out about 120 ¼" (6mm) circles with the circle cutter. Remove the waste clay from around the circles and bake the circles in the same way as the mosaic tiles. After baking, slide a knife blade under the circles to remove them from the tile.

STEP 6: prepare the wood pieces

Sand the edges of the wood to remove rough areas. Tack a hanging loop to the top back of the larger wood rectangle. The two pieces of wood will be tacked together after the mosaic is made.

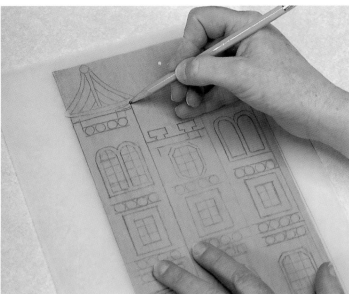

▶▶

STEP 7: trace the design

Trace the templates onto tracing paper and transfer the design to the wood pieces. Be sure to mark the area at the bottom of the large rectangle where the sconce base will be attached—and which should not be covered with mosaic pieces.

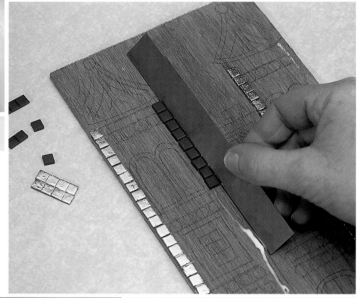

STEP 8: begin the mosaic

Spread a line of PVA glue along the vertical lines at the edges of the towers and apply a line of gold leaf tiles along the tops and left-hand edge of each outer tower. Glue a dark brown line along the right-hand edge of the left-hand tower. Use a tissue blade to straighten the lines while the glue is still wet.

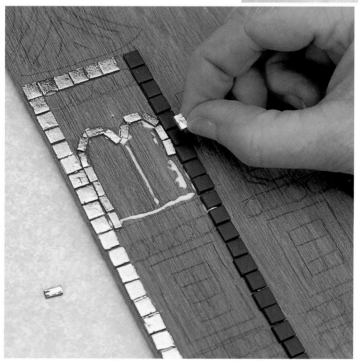

STEP 9: begin the upper arched windows

Apply a line of glue to the outline of the upper arched windows. Cut some gold leaf tiles into thirds, lengthwise, to make narrow strips. Press these onto the glue, curving them to fit around the top of each arch.

STEP 10: fill the arched windows

Apply glue to the center of the arched windows and fill with two vertical lines of navy blue tiles, cutting them to fit if necessary and trimming the top tiles to fit against the curved arches.

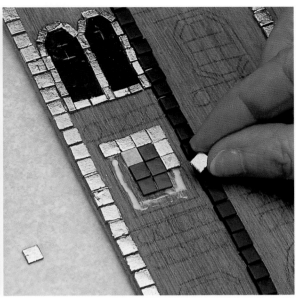

STEP 11: make the blue-green jewel windows

Apply glue to the rectangular window and apply five blue-green tiles in a block in the center, with one pale blue-green tile at the top left for a highlight. Apply a row of gold leaf tiles around the blue-green ones.

STEP 12: make the blue pearl jewel windows

Spread glue on the outlined area of the oval window. Press on blue pearl tiles to fill the inner rectangle, placing one pale blue-green tile at the top left corner. Trim off the outer corner of each corner tile to make the oval shape. Outline with gold leaf tiles cut into thirds, angling the corner pieces to follow the oval shape.

STEP 13: make the hanging chains

Cut five gold leaf tiles into quarters and glue these, set diagonally, along the lines hanging from the top of the large central arch.

STEP 14:
make the hanging pearl drops

Cut three of the pearl circles into pearl-drop shapes and glue one of these at the bottom of each chain. Glue another quarter gold leaf tile just under each pearl drop.

STEP 15: make the central arched window

Glue a vertical line of gold leaf tiles down the left-hand side of the central tower and a line of dark brown tiles down the right-hand side. Cut gold leaf tiles into thirds, lengthwise, and use these to outline the sides and top of the arch. They will fit tightly against the lines of vertical tiles on either side. Glue a line of whole gold leaf tiles along the bottom of the window.

STEP 16: fill in the window background

Fill in the area inside the window with navy blue tiles, cutting them to fit around the chains and pearls.

STEP 17: apply the pearl circles

Apply glue along the outlines that mark the position of the pearl circles and glue a line of four pearl circles onto each, spacing them evenly. Complete the windows and pearl circles in the other towers in the same way.

STEP 18: make the roofs

Cut some dark brown tiles into thirds, lengthwise, and glue these to the outlines of the tower roof. Glue another line of narrow dark brown tiles down the center line of the roof.

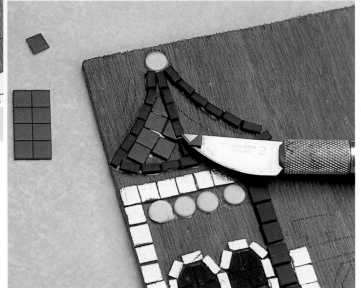

STEP 19: fill in the roof tiles

Glue copper tiles, placed at an angle and cut to fit, to fill the area inside the roof outline. Glue a pearl circle to the top of the tower.

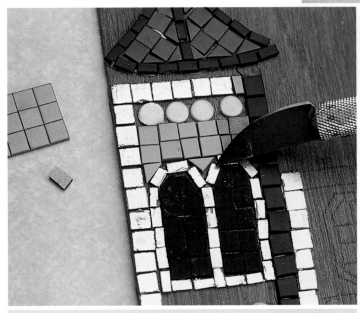

STEP 20: fill in the golden brickwork

▸▸

Apply glue to the remaining areas of the tower and press on lines of gold and golden brown tiles in horizontal rows. Place the golden brown pieces at the right-hand end of each row to suggest shadow. Cut pieces to fit as necessary around the windows and pearl rows. Remember to leave the strip at the bottom of the mosaic untiled so that it can be attached to the sconce base.

STEP 21:
fill remaining towers and battlements

STEP 22: **make the sky**

Complete the right-hand and central towers in the same way as the left-hand tower. Glue a half gold leaf tile in place on each side of the top of the central tower. Glue two more gold leaf tiles on top of each of these for the battlements. Fill in the space under the tower roofs with golden brown tiles cut to shape.

Glue horizontal lines of blue-gray tiles to fill in the sky behind the tops of the towers. Cut the tiles to fit around the roofs and battlements.

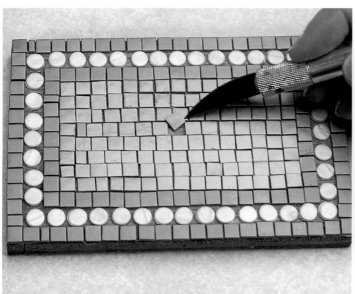

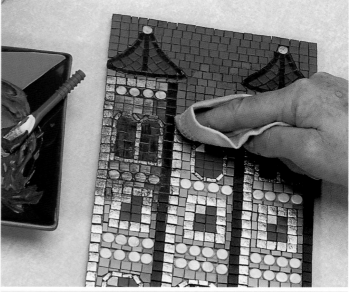

STEP 23: **tile the sconce base**

STEP 24: **grout the mosaic**

Apply glue to the smaller piece of wood and glue a row of gold tiles all around the outside edge. Now glue a row of pearl circles inside this, spacing them so that they fit evenly. Glue another row of gold tiles inside the pearl circles and finally fill in the central area with rows of gold tiles.

For added protection for the gold leaf tiles, paint them with another coat of gloss varnish. Leave the mosaic for several hours to allow the glue and varnish to dry thoroughly. Mix some black paint into a small cup of grout to make a middle gray. Use this to grout the mosaics, following the instructions on page 25.

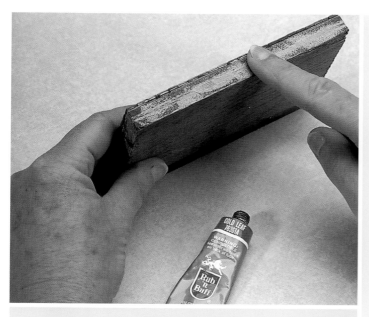

STEP 25: gild the bare wood

Rub gold Rub 'n Buff over all the edges of the wood except the back edge of the sconce base (or paint them with gold paint). If you wish, you can apply gold mosaic tiles to the edges instead.

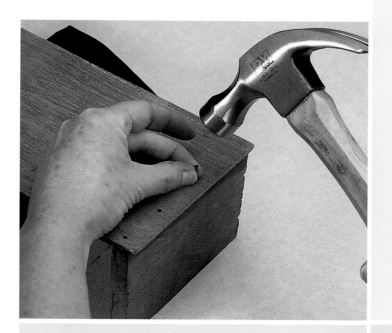

STEP 26: assemble the sconce

Apply wood glue to the back edge of the sconce base. Press this onto the bare wood strip along the bottom front of the main mosaic and hammer tacks into the back to secure. **Optional:** This is easier to do if you support the sconce on a brick padded with fabric.

▸▸**add a candle:** Place a candle on the sconce base and light it to see the full glory of the Byzantine design sparkling in the candlelight! Use a sturdy pillar candle, about 6" (15cm) tall and 2"–2½" (5cm–6cm) in diameter so that it stands solidly without support. Alternatively, place several votive candles in small glass jars on the base.

garden mosaic key holder

Glass millefiori pieces have been used in mosaics for centuries. This beautiful project combines classical mosaic techniques with polymer clay millefiori. If you have not encountered polymer clay millefiori before, you are in for a treat! Basic millefiori techniques are described on page 19. The instructions here will show you how to make a glorious variety of flower and leaf canes that are then sliced and applied to the mosaic for the flowering plants in the garden. The mosaic is used to decorate a key holder, but it could be adapted to make a beautiful box lid or picture instead. ▪

materials

- 2-ounce (or 65g) blocks of polymer clay: 2 blocks of leaf green, 2 blocks of white, 1 block of blue, 1 block of golden yellow, ½ block of crimson, ½ block of dark brown, ¼ block of beige *(Premo! Ecru)*, ¼ block of black, ¼ block of orange, ¼ block of purple, ⅛ block of gold *(see mixtures below)*
- pasta machine *(or roller and wood strips)*
- ceramic baking tiles
- pine key holder, about 8" (20cm) high in the center and 12" (30cm) wide
- graph paper
- darning needle
- tissue blade
- tracing paper and pencil
- transfer paper *(optional)*
- PVA glue
- tile grout
- brown or gray acrylic paint
- grout spreader
- soft cloth
- wax furniture polish

mixtures

- **sky blue** = ¼ block of white + ⅛ block of blue
- **pale sky blue** = ¼ block of white + half the sky blue mixture
- **dark leaf green** = ¼ block of leaf green + ⅛ block of blue
- **pale leaf green** = ⅛ of the dark leaf green mixture + ⅛ block of white
- **pale rose** = ¼ block of white + 1/16 block of crimson
- **dark gray** = ⅛ block of black + ⅛ block of white
- **golden brown** = ⅛ block of gold + ⅛ block of dark brown

preparation

- **tiles:** Roll the sky blue and pale sky blue clay mixtures into sheets and follow the instructions on page 24 to make and bake ¼" (6mm) mosaic tiles. Make ¼" (6mm) mosaic tiles from ¼ block of leaf green.

Enlarge pattern at 170% to bring to full size.

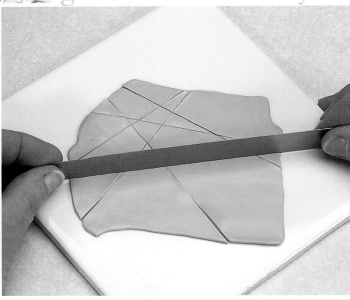

STEP 1: make the crazy paving tiles

Roll the ¼ block of beige clay into a sheet on a ceramic tile. Cut across the sheet at random angles to make crazy paving tiles. Leave on the tile, bake as usual, then separate the tiles when cool.

STEP 2: begin the simple leaf cane

Make a golden yellow and leaf green Skinner blend using ¼ block of each color (see page 17). Roll up the sheet with the yellow in the center, reduce to lengthen the cane to about 5" (13cm) long (see page 19) and cut in half.

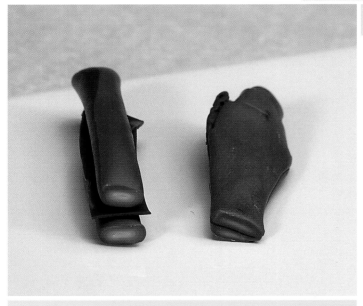

STEP 3: reduce the cane

Sandwich a thin sheet of blue lengthwise between the two halves and press the cane into a teardrop cross section. Pull to reduce (see page 19) until it is about ⅜" (10mm) thick.

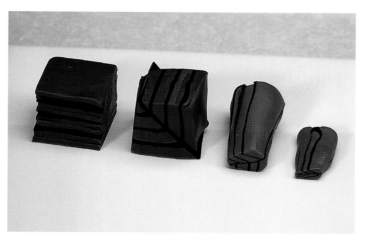

STEP 4: make the veined rose leaf cane

Roll a ¼ block of leaf green into a sheet about ⅛" (3mm) thick (or the thickest setting on your pasta machine). Roll a small black sheet as thin as possible. Cut rectangular pieces from the sheets about 1" (2.5cm) square. Stack these into a loaf, two thick leaf green sheets alternating with a black sheet. Cut the loaf lengthwise, diagonally. Assemble again, flipping one half so the lines make a chevron shape, and sandwiching a thin sheet of black between the two halves. Press into a cane with a leaf-shaped cross section and reduce as before.

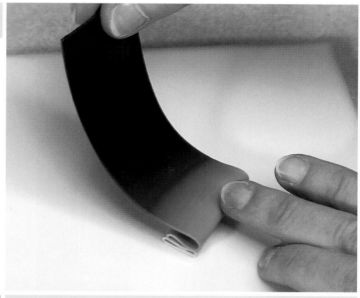

STEP 5: begin the variegated leaf cane

Make a Skinner blend using ⅛ block each of crimson, leaf green and white (see page 17). Roll out the blended sheet, thinly, and trim it into a rectangle. Starting with the white end, fold the sheet into concertina folds 1" (2.5cm) wide, keeping each fold the same width as the previous ones as you work upward. This will make a graded loaf 1" (2.5cm) wide, about 2" (5cm) long and ½" (13mm) high.

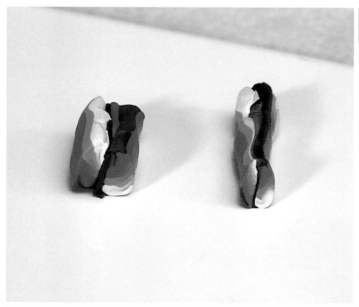

STEP 6: reduce the variegated leaf cane

Pull the loaf to reduce it until it is about 4" (10cm) long. Cut the loaf in half, flip one half, and sandwich both halves together again with a thin sheet of crimson between them. Shape the cane into a leaf-shaped cross section. Reduce as before.

▶▶

STEP 7: make the striped leaf cane

Roll the dark leaf green and the pale leaf green mixtures into thick sheets. Cut rectangles as for the veined rose leaf, and stack a loaf, alternating a sheet of each color. Cut the loaf lengthwise, diagonally. Reassemble, flipping one half. Press into a leaf-shaped cross section and reduce. Try making more leaf canes, using these techniques and varying the green colors.

STEP 8: make the rose cane

Roll the pale rose mixture into a sheet and trim to about 2" x 4" (5cm x 10cm). Roll out and cut a sheet of crimson clay of the same size. Place the crimson sheet on top of the pale rose sheet and roll up like a jelly roll (Swiss roll). Reduce the cane until it is about ¼" (6mm) diameter.

STEP 9: make the blue hyacinth cane

Make a Skinner blend of ⅛ block of blue and ⅛ block of white. Roll up the sheet with the blue in the center. Reduce the cane to about ¼" (6mm) thick and cut into six equal lengths. Stack these into a pyramid, three on the bottom, then two, then one. Reduce the cane to ¼" (6mm) thick by pulling, retaining the pyramid cross section.

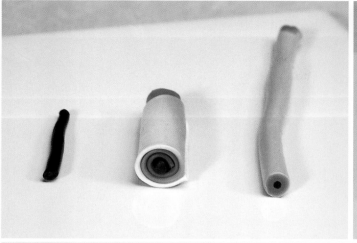

STEP 10: make the hollyhock cane

Make a Skinner blend sheet using ⅛ block of white and ⅛ block of purple. Form a ⅛" (3mm) thick log of purple and lay it on the darker end of the sheet. Roll up with the purple in the middle. Reduce to ¼" (6mm) thick, cut a 2" (5cm) length, and further reduce one end of this so that you can cut slices of varying diameters. The smallest slices should be about ⅛" (3mm) across.

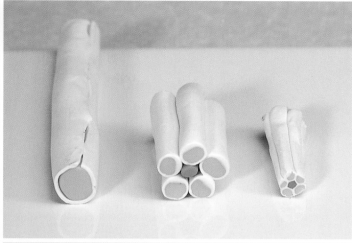

STEP 11: make the yellow daisy cane

Form a ½" (13mm) thick log of golden yellow clay, 2" (5cm) long. Roll out a very thin sheet of white clay and wrap this around the yellow log. Reduce the cane until it is about ¼" (6mm) thick. Cut into five equal lengths. Form an orange log, about ⅛" (3mm) thick, and assemble the cane with the orange log in the center and the yellow logs around the outside. Pull the cane to reduce it to about ¼" (6mm) thick. White daisies are made in the same way as the yellow daisies, using dark gray to wrap the white log, with a black log in the center.

STEP 12: make the sunflower cane

Form a ¾" (20mm) thick log of golden yellow clay, 3" (8cm) long. Roll out a very thin sheet of dark brown clay and wrap this around the yellow log. Reduce the cane until it is about ¼" (6mm) thick and press it onto the work surface to give it an oval cross section. Cut into twelve equal lengths about 2" (5cm) long. Form a golden brown log, about ¼" (6mm) thick, and arrange the yellow logs around the outside, points outward. Form a ¼" (6mm) thick log of dark brown and press this into a triangular cross section. Cut lengths to pack between the tips of the petals. Pull the cane to reduce it to about ⅜" (10mm) thick. Further reduce part of the cane to about ⅛" (3mm) thick for smaller sunflowers.

STEP 13: slice and bake the canes

When all the canes are made, use a tissue blade to cut ¹⁄₁₆" (1.5mm) thick slices from each cane. Try to make the slices as even in thickness as possible. You will need about eight to ten flower slices for each clump of flowers and a similar number of leaves. Vary the size of the canes by further reducing some of them and cutting more slices. Place all the cane slices on a tile and bake for 20 minutes.

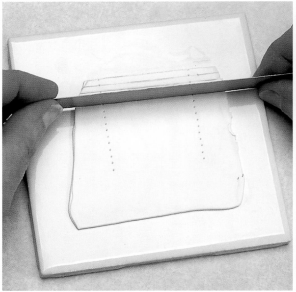

STEP 14:
make white strips for the archway

Roll out ⅛ block of white clay on a ceramic tile. Lay a sheet of graph paper over the clay, and prick a line at ⅛" (3mm) intervals. Make another line 2" (5cm) away from the first. Remove the graph paper and use your blade to cut across the pricks to make strips, removing the waste clay from around them. Leave the clay on the tile and bake for 20 minutes.

STEP 15: transfer the design

Trace the template onto tracing paper and transfer the design to the key holder frame by penciling the back as before or using transfer paper. The outlines for the clumps of flowers are only for guidance, and you can place the flower and leaf canes yourself to best advantage for fit and design.

STEP 16: create the rose arch

Spread a thin coat of PVA glue over the arch and press on rose cane slices and rose leaf slices. Glue the white strips onto the lines of the arch, cutting them to fit against the roses and leaves as necessary.

STEP 17: cover the white gate

Spread glue over the gate area and cut six white strips all the same length for the gate uprights. Press these down onto the traced outline, ensuring that they are evenly spaced. Cut short pieces of white strip to fit between the uprights for the two crossbars and glue into place.

STEP 18: add the sunflowers

Spread glue over a sunflower outline and press on the flower cane slices. Arrange striped leaf slices around the flowers, angled outward in a natural way.

STEP 19: add the hyacinths

Glue the hyacinth flower slices on the outlines and then arrange the simple leaf slices around them. The hyacinths look best if the leaves are placed below the flowers.

STEP 20: add the hollyhocks

Glue the hollyhocks in upright spikes of decreasing sizes. Glue striped leaf slices around the base of each spike. Continue gluing the flower and leaf slices onto the design in the positions indicated.

STEP 21: add the paving tiles

Spread glue over the foreground area and apply the beige crazy paving tiles, angling them to fit against each other and cutting them as necessary. The crazy paving should be cut to fit into the spaces under the bottom leaves of the plants.

STEP 22: begin adding the sky

Glue the pale sky blue tiles in rows above the tops of the flowers and in the archway, using the horizontal guidelines to keep the lines straight. Cut the tiles to fit where they meet the flowers and the edge of the mosaic.

STEP 23: complete the sky

Continue upward in rows, changing to the sky blue tiles as seen in the finished project on page 67. The tiles need to be cut to fit against the upper edge of the key holder and around the upper leaves. Cut leaf green mosaic tiles to fit in the spaces between the leaves and glue in place.

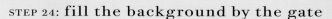

STEP 24: **fill the background by the gate**

Cut pale sky blue tiles to fit in the spaces between the gate uprights. Use leaf green tiles for the spaces lower down the gate to suggest a lawn beyond the gate. Fill all the remaining large spaces with pale sky blue for the upper part and leaf green for the lower part of the mosaic.

STEP 25: **grout the mosaic**

Leave the mosaic to dry thoroughly. Grout the mosaic with white grout (see page 25). For a stronger effect, you can mix brown or gray paint into the grout to make a darker grout for the area around the plants.

▸▸**mosaic vistas:** The finished mosaic shows how pleasing mosaic pictures can be. You really feel you could walk through the gate into another garden beyond! Try using different color combinations for the flower and leaf canes: pastel colors predominate in the colors given here, but you could use stronger colors such as hot reds, purple and deep blue with a vivid green for the leaves to suggest a tropical garden.

I f you enjoy miniatures, then micromosaics will fascinate you—tiny pieces of colored semiprecious stones, applied to a background in a pattern or image and made into little box lids and jewelry. Often, you can hardly see that the image is made up of hundreds of tiny fragments.

The Romans first perfected the technique two thousand years ago, and the craft

micro
mosaics

has been continued by many cultures through the ages. True micromosaic is extremely difficult and time-consuming, but today, thanks to polymer clay, it is possible to simulate this exquisite art form with very little effort.

I have found that the quickest and easiest way to make micromosaics with polymer clay is to use soft-on-soft appliqué: Tiny slices of soft clay are applied to a soft clay background with the point of a knife. This means that your fingers need never touch the clay (they would be far too big to use as tools anyway). The technique requires a little practice (see page 20), but I have found that students in my workshops can achieve excellent results remarkably quickly. You have to approach the technique as if you were embroidering a picture where, instead of using colored thread and a needle, you use soft clay and a knife. ■

basic tips

▸▸ Use a strong, firm clay such as Premo! Sculpey or Fimo Classic for best results.

▸▸ Leach the clay if it is soft (see page 15). Appliqué is much easier with firm clay, and you will achieve crisper results.

▸▸ You will need a craft knife with a curved blade as shown on page 12. This type of blade is readily available from arts and crafts stores. A straight-edged blade is almost impossible to use successfully for this technique.

celtic beast barrette

I first encountered Celtic designs when I worked as an archaeological illustrator, drawing the fabulous jewelry that had been excavated from Anglo-Saxon sites in Britain. I was intrigued to find that many of the flowing motifs actually consisted of twining animals and birds, barely visible to the uninitiated eye. The design for this barrette was inspired by a beautiful seventh-century silver and gold brooch found in Hunterston in Scotland. ■

materials

- 2-ounce (or 65g) blocks of polymer clay: ½ block of beige *(Premo! Ecru)*; ½ block of white; 1/16 block each of black, blue, blue-green, crimson, purple; scrap of yellow *(see mixtures below)*
- pasta machine *(or roller and wood strips)*
- ceramic baking tile
- tracing paper and pencil
- craft knife with curved blade
- darning needle
- tissue blade
- epoxy glue *(or superglue)*
- barrette back

mixtures

- **mauve** = ⅛ block of white + 1/16 block of purple
- **pale blue** = ⅛ block of white + 1/16 block of blue
- **pale blue-green** = ⅛ block of white + 1/16 block of blue-green
- **pink** = ⅛ block of white + 1/16 block of crimson

This is an enlarged detail from the above brooch.

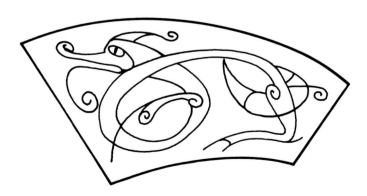

The pattern appears here at full size.

STEP 1: make the barrette base

Trace the template and cut it out. Roll out the beige clay into a sheet ⅛"
(3mm) thick and place on the ceramic tile. Lay the traced template over
the clay and cut out the shape. Use the needle to prick the design
through the tracing paper onto the clay.

STEP 2: apply the black outline

Roll out a sheet of black clay, ¹⁄₁₆" (1.5mm) thick, and cut a strip just
over ¹⁄₁₆" (1.5mm) wide. Lay this strip on the tile beside your working
hand, angled so you can cut slices easily. Cut slices from the strip and
using the appliqué technique (see page 20), apply them to the pricked
line, aligning the tiny rectangles along the lines.

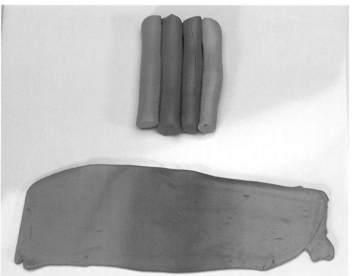

STEP 3: apply the white infill

When the black outline is complete, roll out a sheet of white clay, ¹⁄₁₆"
(1.5mm) thick and cut a ¹⁄₁₆" (1.5mm) wide strip. Cut and apply slices in
the same way as for the black tesserae, filling in the area between the
black outlines. If you have narrow spaces to fill, you can cut narrower
slices by flattening the clay strip slightly before slicing.

STEP 4: mix the rainbow blend

Form the pink, mauve, pale blue and pale blue-green mixtures into ¼"
(6mm) thick logs and press these together in the order shown. Follow
the instructions on page 18 to make a multiple strip blend. This is a
quick way of mixing lots of colors that grade from one color to the next.
Finally, roll out the clay blend into a ¹⁄₁₆" (1.5mm) thick sheet.

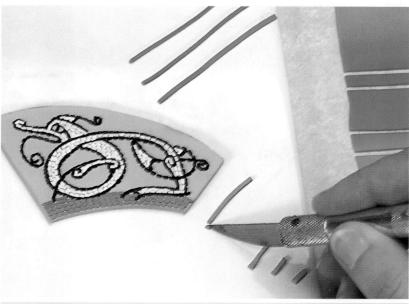

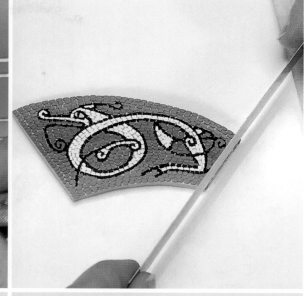

STEP 5: begin the background

Press a small oval of yellow clay onto the eye and apply a strip of black for a pupil. Cut ¹⁄₁₆" (1.5mm) wide clay strips from the blended sheet to give a series of strips that grade through the different colors. Starting at the base of the barrette, apply slices of pale blue-green in a horizontal row along the bottom. Repeat to make two more rows, then apply slices from a strip that is a little more blue for the next row.

STEP 6: finish the background

Continue upward in horizontal rows, grading the colors from pale blue-green, through pale blue, mauve and pink. When the background is complete, trim the sides of the piece with a tissue blade. Gently pat over the mosaic with your finger to consolidate all the little slices.

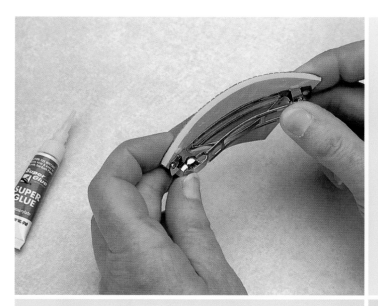

STEP 7: attach the barrette

Bake the mosaic on the tile for 20 to 30 minutes. When cool, remove from the tile and glue the barrette to the back of the mosaic with epoxy glue (or superglue), flexing the clay to fit the curve of the barrette.

▶▶ **barrettes and more:** This barrette can be made in a variety of lovely color schemes. You could use a rainbow of primary colors for the background instead of the pastels suggested. The mosaic panel can also be used to decorate the front of a notebook. Cover the book in coordinating handmade paper and glue the panel to the front.

mogul miniature pin

The Mogul emperors ruled in India between the sixteenth and nineteenth centuries and left a legacy of extraordinary artwork, including beautiful miniature paintings. This design is based on the exquisite horses that were often depicted in those miniatures. Gold clay, enhanced with gold paste, is used as a background for the mosaic, which is quick to make because it does not have background tiling. This mosaic is much finer than the Celtic Beast Barrette project, and you will need a steady hand to position the slices, but the result gives exquisite detail. ■

materials

- 2-ounce (or 65g) blocks of polymer clay: ½ block of gold, 1/16 block of beige *(Premo! Ecru)*, scraps of copper, leaf green, orange, pearl *(see mixtures below)*
- pasta machine *(or roller and wood strips)*
- ceramic baking tile
- tracing paper and pencil
- stiff cardstock
- darning needle
- craft knife with curved blade
- gold Rub 'n Buff
- fine paintbrush
- soft cloth
- epoxy glue *(or superglue)*
- brooch back

mixtures

- **green pearl** = ⅜" (10mm) ball of pearl + trace of leaf green
- **orange pearl** = ⅜" (10mm) ball of pearl + trace of orange

The pattern appears here at full size.

STEP 1: prepare the mosaic base

Roll out a sheet of gold clay, about ⅛" (3mm) thick, on the ceramic tile. Trace the template outline onto the cardstock and cut out the shape. Lay the cardstock onto the clay and cut around it, holding your knife vertically. The stiff cardstock makes it easier to get a neat edge. Trace the template design onto tracing paper, lay this over the clay, and prick the design with the needle.

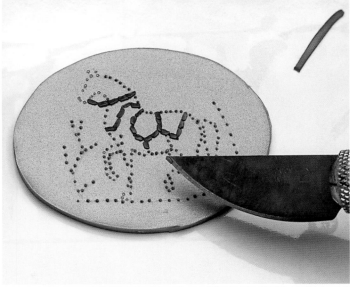

STEP 2: apply the reins and saddle outlines

Roll out a pea-size piece of copper clay into a sheet, ¹⁄₃₂" (1mm) thick. Cut a strip ¹⁄₃₂" (1mm) wide. Cut and apply slices along the lines of the reins, saddle and saddle blanket.

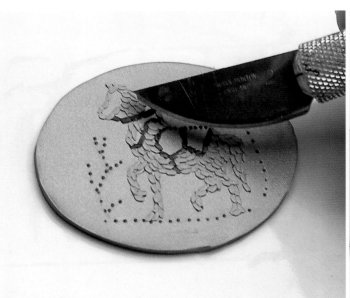

STEP 3: make the horse

Roll out a piece of beige clay in the same way and cut a ¹⁄₃₂" (1mm) wide strip. Cut and apply slices along the outline of the horse. Continue to apply beige slices inside these outlines, filling the space and aligning the slices along the lines of the body.

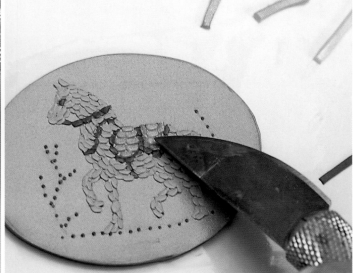

STEP 4: finish the saddle

Using ¹⁄₃₂" (1mm) strips as before, apply orange pearl slices to the area inside the saddle outline, and green pearl and pearl slices to the blanket. A single slice of copper makes the horse's eye.

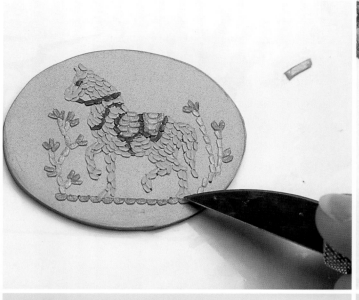

STEP 5: add the grass and plants

Apply a line of green pearl to the marked line below the horse. Apply pearl slices for the stems of the plants, and green pearl slices for the foliage. Pat over the mosaic to consolidate the slices and bake for 15 minutes on the tile.

STEP 6: gild the background

When the mosaic is cool, remove it from the tile and brush gold Rub 'n Buff over the background to highlight it, using a fine brush to reach into the corners between the mosaic slices. Allow to dry, then buff to a shine.

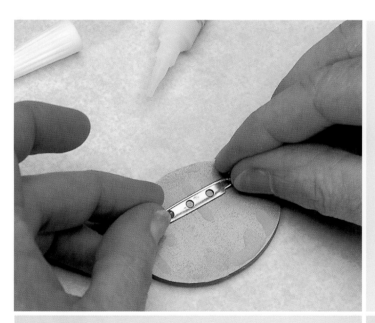

STEP 7: attach the pin

Using epoxy glue (or superglue), glue the pin to the back of the mosaic. It is best to glue the pin horizontally and to the upper part of the mosaic so that it will not sag when it is worn.

▶▶ **royal accessory:** The finished pin is fit for a Mogul prince or princess to wear! The colors given are typical of the miniature painting of this period—mellow apricots and copper colors complement the soft greens and gold. Try using colors such as blues and purples on a silver background for a completely different look.

greek temple snuffbox

This polymer clay replica of a nineteenth-century micromosaic snuffbox is remarkably like the original box, which is extremely valuable and made with gold and semiprecious stones! Although micromosaics in classical style were developed by the Romans, they became very popular again in the nineteenth century when the exquisite craftsmanship of the time gave superb detail. The micromosaic on the lid of this little box depicts a Greek temple by the sea, and like the original, the tiny elongated tesserae are positioned to enhance the flow of the design. Millefiori slices frame the image, again, just like the original. ■

materials

- 2-ounce (or 65g) blocks of polymer clay: 1 block of beige *(Premo! Ecru)*; ½ block of black; ¼ block of white; 1/16 block each of blue, copper, dark brown, golden yellow, gray, green, leaf green *(see mixtures below)*
- pasta machine *(or roller and wood strips)*
- ceramic baking tile
- tracing paper and pencil
- tissue blade
- darning needle
- craft knife with curved blade
- piece of fabric *[or textured paper towels (kitchen paper)]*
- fine sandpaper
- superglue
- toothpick *[(cocktail stick) or wooden BBQ skewer]*
- gold Rub 'n Buff *(or gold acrylic paint)*
- fine paintbrush
- PVA glue

mixtures

Use a ½" (13mm) ball of each color.

- **blue-gray** = 1 blue + 1 gray
- **pale yellow** = 1 white + 1 golden yellow

skinner blends

Make each blend using a ½" (13mm) ball of each color.

- **blue / white**
- **copper / golden yellow**
- **dark brown / beige**
- **green / golden yellow**

preparation

- **skinner blends:** Make the Skinner blends listed at left; they will be very small but you need only very small amounts. Roll the blends and mixtures into 1/32" (1mm) thick sheets.

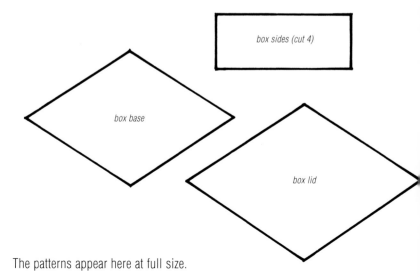

box sides (cut 4)

box base

box lid

The patterns appear here at full size.

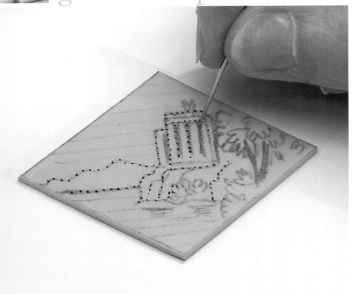

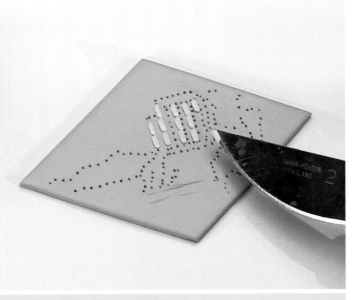

STEP 1: make the mosaic base

Roll out a sheet of beige, about 1/10" (2.5mm) thick. Place on a ceramic tile. Trace and cut out the template, lay it on the clay, and cut out the shape with a tissue blade. Prick the design through the tracing paper with the needle.

STEP 2: make the pillars

Cut 1/16" (1.5mm) wide strips from the pale yellow sheet. Flatten the strip slightly, and cut and apply long slices to the pillars of the temple (see page 20 for instructions on appliqué technique).

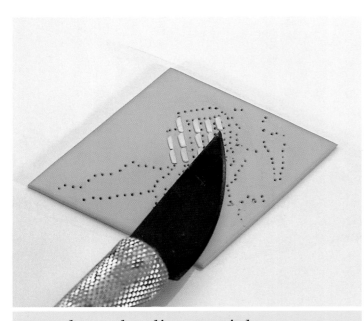

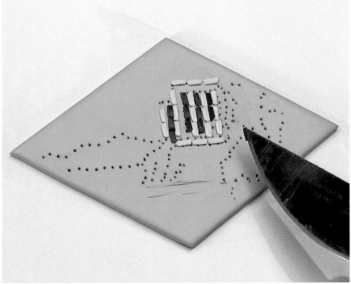

STEP 3: keep the slices straight

Take care that the long slices that make up the pillars are kept vertical and in line: Always cut each slice with the tip of your knife so that it is just visible behind the blade as you apply it.

STEP 4: apply the temple shadows

Cut strips from the dark brown end of the blended dark brown and beige sheet, same as you did with the pale yellow. Flatten the strip and cut long thin slices to apply to the dark spaces between the pillars.

STEP 5: finish the temple

Use slices of a light brown strip, cut from halfway along the same blend. Apply it to the central part of the pillars between the pale yellow and dark brown.

STEP 6: add the cliff

Cut several different-colored strips from the copper and golden yellow blend and the dark brown. Cut and apply long slices as before, angling them down the slope of the cliff, varying the colors for a pleasing effect.

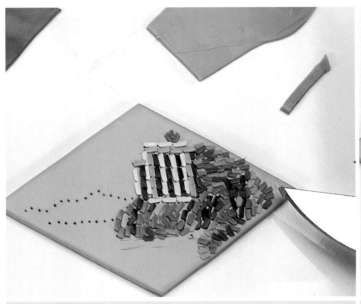

STEP 7: add the foliage

Cut different-colored strips from the green and golden yellow blend. Roll out a small sheet of leaf green clay, ¹⁄₃₂" (1mm) thick, and cut a strip. Cut and apply slices of these different greens to make the trees behind the temple and the grass in the foreground. Apply three small leaves on top of the temple. Apply slices of dark brown to suggest tree trunks.

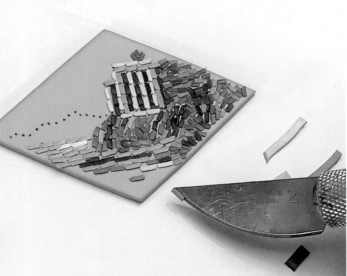

STEP 8: add the water

Cut strips from the blue and white blend, flatten them, and cut and apply slices of these in horizontal lines for the water. Apply a line of blue-gray for the water and another of white for reflection.

STEP 9: add the hills

Use a middle brown from the brown and beige blend for the strips. Cut and apply slices, following the lines of the hills.

STEP 10: add the sky

Cut and apply long slices from flattened strips of pale yellow at the horizon, grading through white to pale blue. All the strips for the sky should be horizontal. When you have finished the mosaic, pat over the surface to consolidate all the applied pieces.

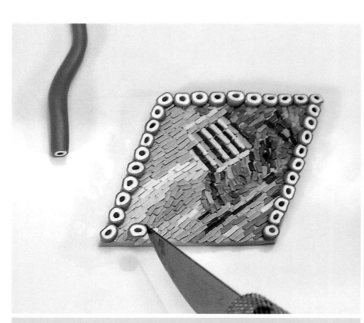

STEP 11: prepare the millefiori cane

Form a ⅛" (3mm) thick log of dark brown, about 2" (5cm) long. Wrap this in a ⅛" (3mm) thick sheet of white, then in a 1/16" (1.5mm) thick sheet of blue-gray. Reduce to ⅛" (3mm) thick (see page 19). Set aside to cool and harden slightly (or place in the refrigerator) before slicing. Slice the cane into 1/16" (1.5mm) thick slices, as evenly as possible, and apply them along the mosaic's edges. Bake the mosaic on the ceramic tile for 20 minutes.

STEP 12: begin the box

Trace and cut out the box templates. Roll out black clay to 1/16" (1.5mm) thick. Lay a sheet of fabric [or paper towel (kitchen paper)] onto the clay and roll the surface (or pass the sheet through pasta machine) again. Peel off the fabric to reveal the textured surface.

STEP 13: make the box sides

Lay the textured clay on the ceramic tile and use the template and tissue blade to cut out the box sides as accurately as possible. Remove the waste clay and leave the pieces on the tile for baking.

STEP 14: make the box lid and base

Roll out some beige clay ⅛" (3mm) thick and lay it on the tile. Cut out the box base and lid. Bake all the box pieces on their tiles for 30 minutes.

STEP 15: trim the pieces of the box ▶▶

Lay out all the box pieces with the sides adjacent to the base. Trim the sides so that they are exactly the same length as the sides of the base. Sand any rough areas.

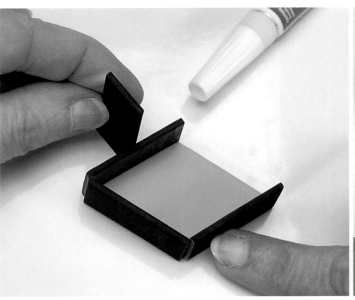

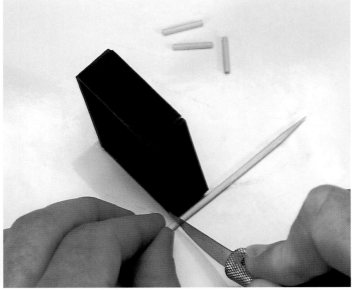

STEP 16: **assemble the box**

Apply a line of superglue to the bottom of each side and press this onto the box base. To ensure that the sides are vertical, push one of the other box sides against the one being glued.

STEP 17: **cut the corner pieces**

Use the box sides as a guide to cut lengths of toothpick (cocktail stick) for the corners. They should be exactly the same height as the box sides. Sand the cuts smooth.

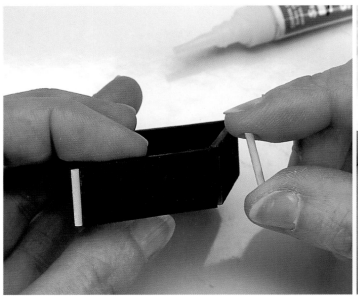

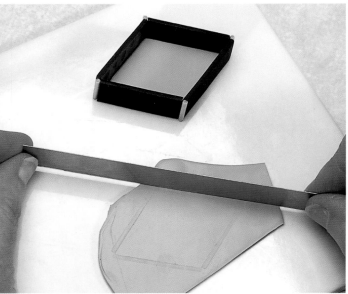

STEP 18: **attach the corners**

Glue the corner pieces in place at each box corner to neaten them. They should fit comfortably into the groove where the sides meet.

STEP 19: **make the lid insert**

Roll out some beige clay on a tile, ⅛" (3mm) thick, and press the completed box onto the soft clay to make an impression. Use the tissue blade to cut along the inside lines to make a lid insert that will fit exactly inside the box. Bake the insert on the tile as before.

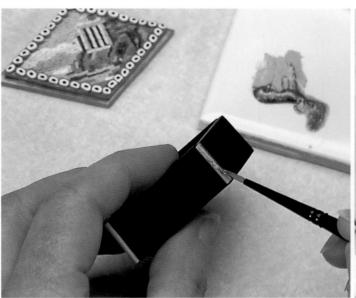

STEP 20: **gild the lid and corners**	STEP 21: **finish the box**
Glue the mosaic onto the beige box lid. Paint the lid and mosaic sides with gold Rub 'n Buff or gold acrylic paint. Paint the corner pieces gold, as well, avoiding getting gold on the black box sides.	Glue the lid insert centrally to the inside of the box lid with PVA glue. This type of glue will allow you to try the lid on the box and reposition the insert, if necessary, to get a good fit.

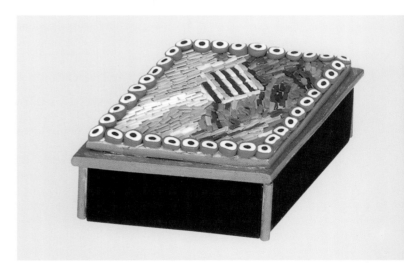

▸▸**vary the details:** The textured black sides of the box provide a pleasing matte contrast to the shiny gold that frames the mosaic picture. For a different look, you can apply gold Rub 'n Buff to the box sides, as well. Try texturing the sides with fine lace for a really opulent look.

Pietre dure is pronounced "pee-etra doora" and means "semiprecious stones" in Italian. It is a type of mosaic that was first developed in Florence in the fifteenth century. Thin slices of semiprecious stones in different colors are cut into shapes and fitted together in a way similar to marquetry in wood. The natural variations in the stone are used to suggest shading and form.

pietre dure
mosaics

During a trip to Florence a few years ago, I was thrilled with the beauty of pietre dure, both antique and modern. I was determined to try to simulate the glorious effect in polymer clay, and after much trial and error, I finally developed the technique shown here. I found that the easiest way to make polymer clay pietre dure is to work with unbaked sheets of clay. These are marbled or mixed into blends and then cut to shape with a sharp knife and inlaid carefully to form the design.

This technique is more challenging than the other mosaic techniques in this book, but the results are really worth the practice. If you have not tried the technique before, work through the projects in the order given here; the easiest projects are given first. ∎

basic techniques

The easiest method of making pietre dure with polymer clay is to roll the clay into sheets and cut out and assemble the shapes while the clay is still soft. This requires a delicate touch, but if you follow a few simple guidelines, it becomes much easier to achieve.

▸▸ basic tips

Here are some basic tips for making polymer clay pietre dure:

▸▸ Firm clay is the easiest to use. If your clay is soft or sticky, leach it before starting the project (see page 15).

▸▸ Always use the same sheet thickness for both the background and the inlay throughout a single pietre dure project.

▸▸ Use a craft knife with a sharp, straight pointed blade when cutting out the pieces to inlay. Hold the knife as vertical as possible so that the sides of the cut are vertical.

▸▸ Cutout pieces should be removed carefully so that the surrounding clay is not distorted. Use the tip of a needle to ease out a corner and then pull out the whole piece.

▸▸ When laying a cutout piece of clay onto a clay sheet to cut out the inlay, first dust talcum powder over the surface of the clay to prevent sticking.

▸▸ Polymer clay pietre dure can be sanded after baking to smooth out any bumps or imperfections (see page 21). Take care not to sand marbled or finely inlaid areas too vigorously or you may remove some of the detail.

▶▶ marbling

Marbled clay is used frequently in pietre dure because the results simulate the lines and swirls of natural and semiprecious stones, such as marble or agate. Do not use a pasta machine for this type of marbling, because you will not be able to produce the distinctive streaks of color required.

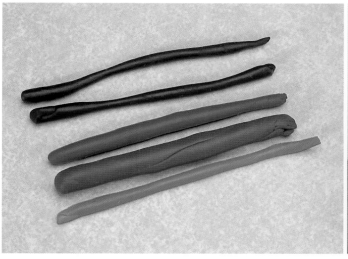

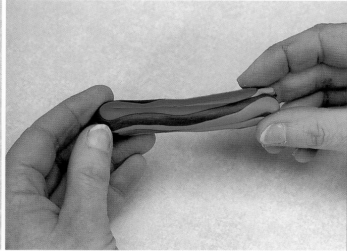

1 FORM THE CLAY COLORS
Form 3" (8cm) logs of the clay colors required for the marbling. The logs can be of varying thickness but should all be the same length.

2 PRESS THE LOGS
Press the colored logs together into a large log and roll it between your hands until it has thinned and doubled in length.

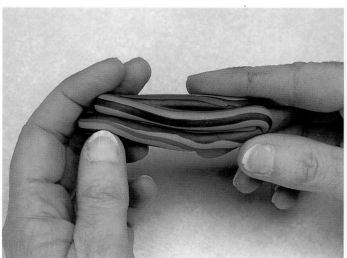

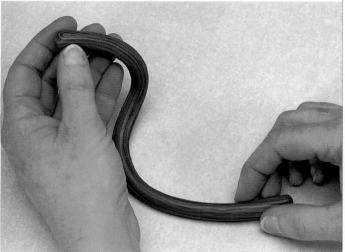

3 ROLL COLOR IN PARALLEL LINES
Fold the log in half, keeping all the lines of colors parallel and being careful not to twist the log. Roll again as before and fold in half again. If rolling causes the lines of color to twist along the log, untwist carefully to make them parallel again.

4 MARBLE THE CLAY
Continue rolling and folding until the streaks are quite fine but still visible. Do not marble for too long, or all the colors will blend into one. You can now fold the log into three, flatten it with your hands, and roll it out it into a sheet, either with a roller or with a pasta machine. If you roll it out across the marbled streaks, the resulting sheet will have swirls and wide bands of color. To obtain a more evenly striped sheet with narrow bands, roll the clay out in the direction of the streaks.

taj mahal necklace

The beauty of the Taj Mahal in India is legendary. This delicate necklace is inspired by the gorgeous pietre dure embellishments that are inlaid into the marble of the building. This project uses cutters to cut out the shapes for inlay, which is a quick and easy way to make simulated pietre dure. A mixture of translucent and white polymer clay simulates the marble, while pearlescent powder on the same clay mixture replicates pearls to make a necklace fit for an Indian princess! ■

Detail of pietre dure mosaic from the Taj Mahal.

materials

- 2-ounce (or 65g) blocks of polymer clay: ½ block of translucent, ¼ block of white, scraps of crimson, leaf green, purple *(see mixtures below)*
- pasta machine *(or roller and wood strips)*
- ceramic baking tile
- tracing paper and pencil
- craft knife with a straight pointed blade
- darning needle
- talcum powder
- leaf cutters, ³⁄₁₆" (5mm)
- flower cutters, ½" (13mm) and ³⁄₁₆" (5mm)
- large tapestry needle
- Pearl Ex powder, white pearl
- soft paintbrush
- gloss varnish
- 16" (41cm) silver-plated chain
- wire cutters
- silver-plated jump rings, two ³⁄₁₆" (5mm) diameter and three ⅛" (3mm) diameter
- 3 silver-plated head pins
- fine-nosed jewelry pliers

mixtures

- **white marble** = ½ block of translucent + ¼ block of white
- **mauve** = equivalent of ¹⁄₁₆ block of white marble mixture + trace of purple
- **pale leaf green** = equivalent of ¹⁄₁₆ block of white marble mixture + trace of leaf green
- **pink** = equivalent of ¹⁄₁₆ block of white marble mixture + trace of crimson

preparation

- **mixtures:** All sheets should be rolled out to the same thickness: about ¹⁄₁₂"(2mm) or a medium setting on the pasta machine.

The pattern appears here at full size.

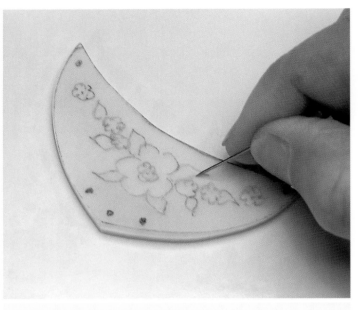

STEP 1: make the background panel

Roll out a sheet of the white marble mixture ½" (2mm) thick and lay the sheet on a ceramic tile. Trace the template and use it to cut out the shape. Hold your knife vertically so that the edges are kept straight.

STEP 2: inscribe the design

Use the darning needle to firmly inscribe over the lines of the design. This will mark the design onto the clay below.

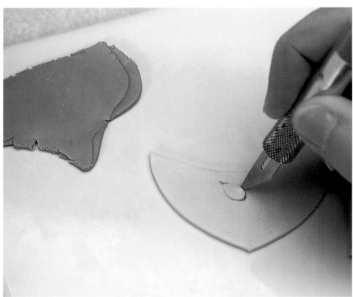

STEP 3: cut out the first leaf

Roll out a sheet of the pale leaf green mixture to the same thickness as the white marble. Using a knife with a pointed blade, cut out one of the four large leaves from the marble panel.

STEP 4: cut out the leaf inlay

Smear a little talcum powder over the leaf green clay and lay the cutout leaf on it. Use this as a pattern to cut out an identical leaf in leaf green. Hold your knife as vertical as possible when cutting.

STEP 5: inlay the leaf

Carefully insert the leaf into the space in the marble panel, pressing
it down lightly until it is flush with the surface. Repeat to inlay the
remaining three large leaves.

STEP 6: cut out the small leaves

Use the ³⁄₁₆" (5mm) leaf cutter to cut out the smaller leaves in the positions indicated on the template. Remove the cutout clay carefully to
avoid damaging the panel.

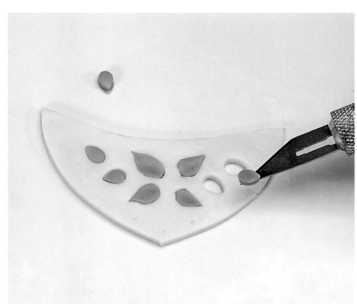

STEP 7: inlay the small leaves

Still using the ³⁄₁₆" (5mm) leaf cutter, cut out four leaves from the pale
leaf green sheet and insert these into the cutout spaces in the panel.

STEP 8: inlay the large mauve flower

Use the ½" (13mm) flower cutter to cut out the flower in the center of
the panel. Roll out a sheet of mauve clay of the same thickness as
before, dust lightly with talcum powder, and cut out the flower to inlay
into the space.

STEP 9: inlay the small flowers

Use the ³⁄₁₆" (5mm) flower cutter to cut out and inlay the small mauve flowers at the corners of the panel. Roll out a sheet of pink clay and cut out and inlay the small pink flowers in the same way.

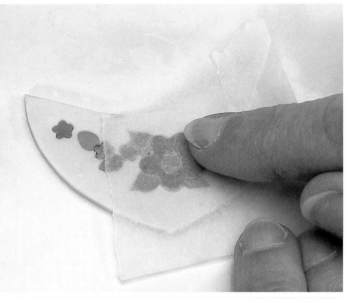

STEP 10: burnish the panel

Lay a piece of tracing paper over the panel and gently burnish with your finger to consolidate the inlay and smooth away any bumps. Take care not to press too hard or the panel will distort, particularly at the edges.

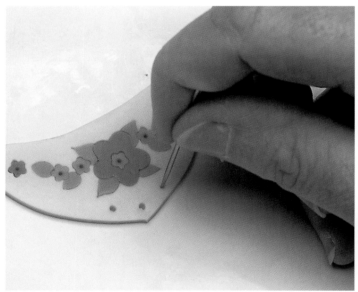

STEP 11: make the holes in the panel

Use a tapestry needle to pierce holes (for the jump rings) in the panel at the points indicated on the template. They need to be large enough for the wire to thread through. Trim the top corners of the panel to round them off. Leave the panel on the tile for baking.

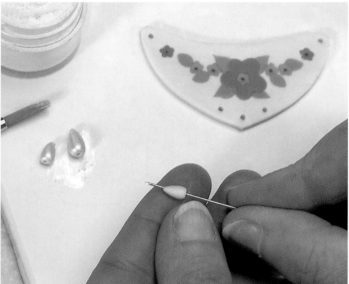

STEP 12: make the pearls

Form one ¼" (6mm) ball of marble clay and two ³⁄₁₆" (5mm) balls. Shape each of these into a teardrop and, holding it in your fingers, pierce lengthwise with the darning needle. Brush each drop with the pearl powder. Bake the panel and pearls for 20 minutes, taking care that the clay does not discolor during the end of the baking time. When the pearls are cool, coat with gloss varnish.

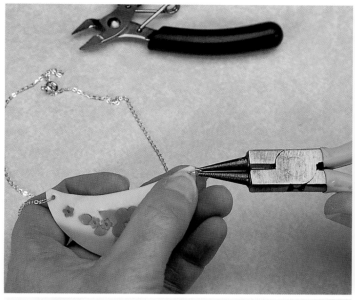

STEP 13: attach the chain

Cut the central 2" (5cm) out of the chain to give 7" (18cm) from the clasp at each end. Attach the ends of the chain to the large jump rings and attach these to the holes at the corners of the pietre dure panel.

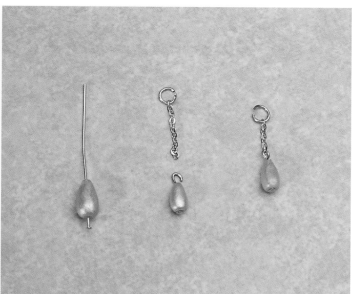

STEP 14: attach the chains to the pearl drops

Cut the leftover chain into one 1" (2.5cm) length and two ½" (13mm) lengths. Thread a head pin through each pearl drop; trim the protruding end to ¼" (6mm). Turn a loop in the end with the fine-nosed pliers. Attach this loop to one end of each chain with the larger pearl drop attached to the longer chain. Attach a small jump ring to the other end of each chain.

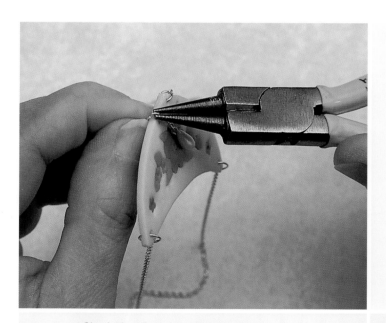

STEP 15: finish the necklace

Use your pliers to squeeze each jump ring onto a hole at the base of the panel, with the larger pearl drop in the center.

▸▸ **taj mahal beauty:** The finished piece has a delicate beauty that is enhanced by the pearl drops. It is important to cut the chains to the correct length so that the central pearl hangs below the outer two. You can adjust the necklace chain as well so that the panel hangs comfortably around the neck of the wearer.

viking ship box

In seventeenth-century Florence, pietre dure was often used to make scenic panels, particularly seascapes. This project uses the nautical theme of a Viking ship for a panel to decorate a wooden box. The lovely streaked effects of the sea and the mountains are achieved by marbling the clay before rolling it out. Colors and mixtures are given for the project, but for this type of scenic mosaic, you can use up all your colored clay scraps in the marbling to get some really exciting results. The template can be enlarged or reduced for other box sizes. ■

materials

- 2-ounce (or 65g) blocks of polymer clay: ½ block of blue, ½ block of pearl, ½ block of white, ¼ block of beige *(Premo! Ecru)*, ¼ block of blue-green, ¼ block of dark brown, ¼ block of gold, ⅛ block of crimson, ¹⁄₁₆ block of red, scraps of gray, purple *(see mixtures below)*
- pasta machine *(or roller and wood strips)*
- ceramic baking tile
- rectangular wooden box, about 9" x 7" x 3" (23cm x 18cm x 8cm)
- tracing paper and pencil
- craft knife with a straight pointed blade
- darning needle
- talcum powder
- long tissue blade *(or carving knife with a long straight blade)*
- tapestry needle
- fine wet/dry sandpaper, 600-grit
- piece of fabric for polishing
- PVA glue

mixtures

- **pale blue** = ¼ block of blue + ¼ block of white
- **pearl blue** = ½ of pale blue mixture + ¼ block of pearl
- **pennant red** = ¹⁄₁₆ block of red + ¹⁄₁₆ block of crimson

preparation

- **mixtures:** All sheets should be rolled out to the same thickness: about ¹⁄₁₂" (2mm) or a medium setting on the pasta machine.

Enlarge pattern at 167% to bring to full size.

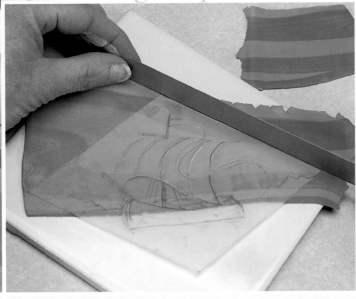

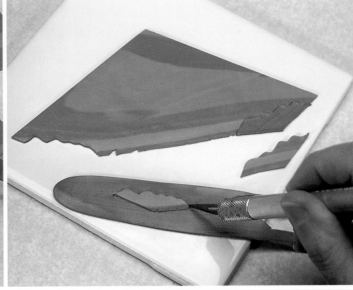

STEP 1: make the sky

Marble a thin log of pearl into each of the pale blue and pearl blue mixtures (see page 89), then marble the two logs together a few times until there are broad streaks. Roll this out into a marbled sheet and lay it on the tile. Trace and cut out the template and lay the sky area over the sheet. Cut around the top edges, leaving the bottom edge untrimmed for now. Save these marbled sky blue trimmings for steps 2 and 4.

STEP 2: make the mountains

Use small quantities of marbled sky blue, gray and purple to make a finely marbled sheet for the mountains. Scribe over the mountain lines of the template with a darning needle, extending the lines below the horizon, and cut out the mountains along the inscribed lines. Dust the marbled sheet with talcum powder, and use the cutout shapes as patterns to cut out the marbled mountain inlays, angling the streaks as shown. Insert these into their respective spaces on the panel.

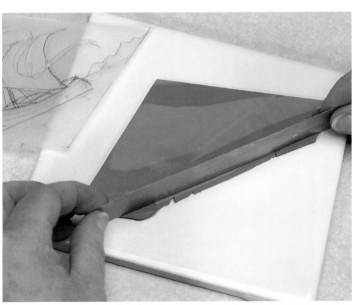

STEP 3: cut the horizon

Lay the template back on the panel and mark the line of the horizon. Use a tissue blade to cut across the panel along this line, and remove the waste clay from below the line.

STEP 4: marble the sea

Marble together ¼" (6mm) thick logs of blue, blue-green and marbled sky blue with ⅛" (3mm) thick logs of crimson and purple until the streaks are fine (see page 89). Roll into a sheet, keeping the stripes aligned.

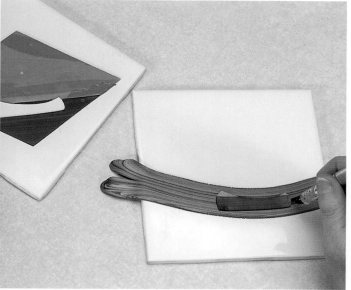

STEP 5: cut out the sea

With the streaks horizontal, cut the top edge into a straight line with a tissue blade and press this up against the horizon line. Align the traced template over the panel and cut out the bottom edges. Inscribe over the template to transfer the ship design onto the clay.

STEP 6: add the ship's hull

Marble together dark brown and gold to make a striped sheet (see page 89). Lay this on the tile, pulling to slightly curve the stripes upward at each end. Cut the main hull area out of the panel and lay the piece onto the striped sheet. The curved stripes will add to the effect of the ship's curved shape.

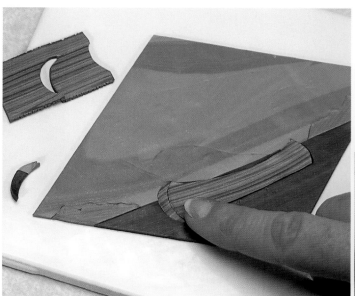

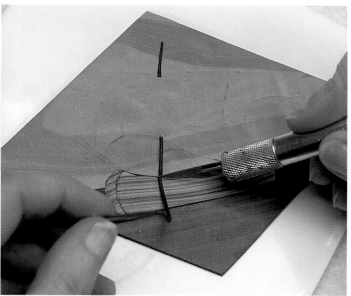

STEP 7: inlay the small hull piece

Cut out the small left-hand hull piece in the same way and inlay with another piece cut from the curved stripes. This time, angle the stripes down to the left to further suggest the curve of the hull.

STEP 8: add the mast

Using the thick tapestry needle, draw deep grooves into the clay along the lines of the mast, overlapping into the area that will be the sail. Form a 1/16" (1.5mm) thick log of dark brown clay and lay this into the grooves, pressing down evenly. Trim the log where it meets the hull.

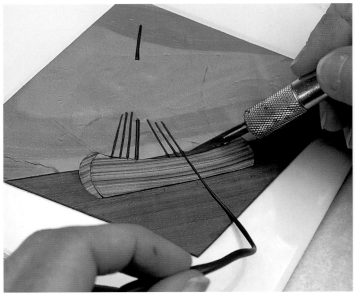

STEP 9: add the ratlines

Inscribe along the lines of the ratlines in the same way and inlay the grooves with 1/32" (1mm) thick threads of dark brown clay, again overlapping into the sail area. The bottom ends of the ratlines and mast should be trimmed carefully where they meet the top line of the hull.

STEP 10: add the sail

Make a broad strip blend of white and gold using a 1/2" (13mm) thick log of white clay and a 1/4" (6mm) thick log of gold clay, both about 2" (5cm) long (see page 18). Cut the sail piece out of the panel and lay this over the blend with the gold part at the bottom right. Cut out and inlay the piece into the sail area on the panel.

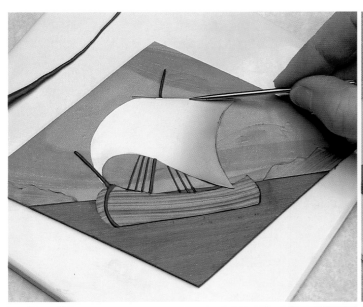

STEP 11: inlay the remaining spars and lines

Inscribe 1/12" (2mm) wide grooves for the bowsprit and the line down the bow. Inlay with 1/12" (2mm) thick logs of dark brown clay as before. Inscribe and inlay the top spar (along the top of the sail) in the same way. Inscribe finer lines for the forestay and backstay and inlay with 1/32" (1mm) threads of dark brown.

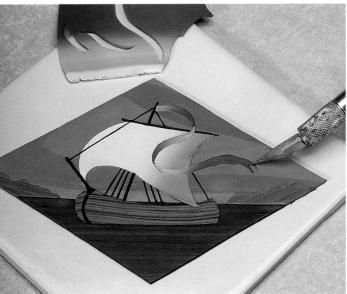

STEP 12: add the pennant

Make a strip blend using pennant red and white. Cut out and inlay the three pieces of the pennant, with the red clay positioned toward the free end of the pennant on each piece. Inlay a few fine horizontal threads of dark brown across the ratlines if you wish.

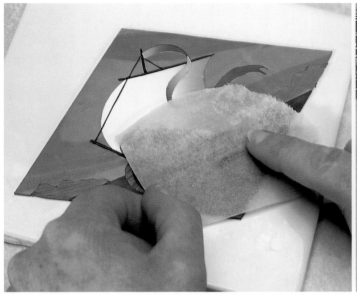

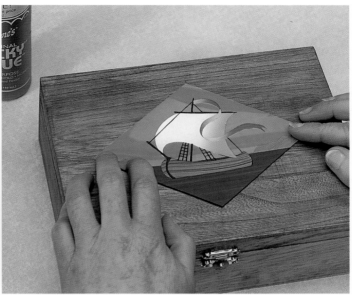

STEP 13: smooth the surface

Lay a piece of tracing paper over the panel and rub over with your finger to smooth the surface. Do not press too hard over the finer lines or they will spread. Trim the edges again if necessary. Bake the piece on the tile for 20 minutes.

STEP 14: finish and mount the panel

While the piece is still warm and still on the ceramic tile, hold it under a gently running faucet and sand the surface to smooth it further. Buff with fabric to give it a gentle shine. Glue the panel to the center of the box lid.

▸▸ **sailing the high seas:** The crimson pennant flying in the wind gives a striking sense of movement to the finished panel. And, if you are willing to part with it, the decorated box makes a lovely gift. As an alternative, the panel could be glued to mounting board and framed to make an unusual picture.

lilies of the valley pin

This delectable pin is made in the style of nineteenth-century pietre dure pieces that often pictured flowers or fruit on a black background. The originals would have been made with marble and chalcedony, but the polymer clay version uses carefully blended colored clays. The tiny pieces that make up this pin mean that this project is quite challenging. Be sure to leach your clay well if it is soft; firm clay is much easier to use for this piece. ■

Detail from pietre dure table, Florence, seventeenth century.

materials

- 2-ounce (or 65g) blocks of polymer clay: ½ block of black, ¼ block of leaf green, ¼ block of white, scraps of blue, golden yellow, gray *(see mixture below)*
- pasta machine *(or roller and wood strips)*
- ceramic baking tile
- tracing paper and pencil
- craft knife with a straight pointed blade
- darning needle
- talcum powder
- tapestry needle
- fine wet/dry sandpaper, 400- and 600-grit
- piece of stiff fabric for polishing
- superglue
- brooch pin

mixture
- **pale leaf green** = ¹⁄₁₆ block of white + ¹⁄₁₆ block of leaf green + trace of golden yellow

preparation

- **mixtures:** All sheets should be rolled out to the same thickness: about ¹⁄₁₂" (2mm) or a medium setting on the pasta machine.

The pattern appears here at full size.

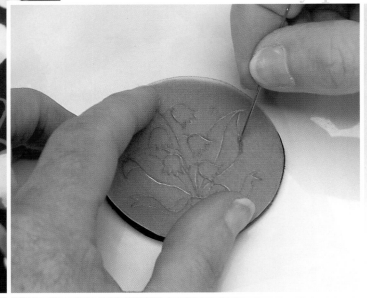

STEP 1: make the background disk

Roll out a sheet of black clay and lay this on a ceramic tile. Trace the template and cut out the circle. Lay this onto the clay and cut round, holding your knife as vertical as possible. Inscribe over the lines of the design with the darning needle to mark the design onto the clay below.

STEP 2: cut out the first leaf

With your knife held vertically, cut out one half of the right-hand leaf. Turn the tile as necessary so that you can cut easily. Remove the cutout piece carefully so that you do not damage the surrounding clay.

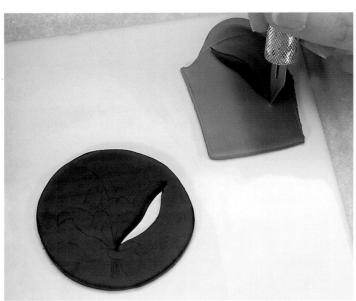

STEP 3: cut the leaf green piece

Make a strip blend using pale leaf green and leaf green (see page 18). Dust the surface of the blend lightly with talcum powder and lay the removed piece onto it, positioning the point of the leaf in the lighter area. Cut round with your knife held vertically.

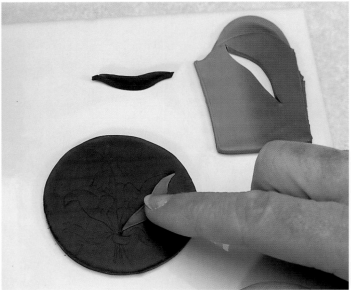

STEP 4: inlay the half leaf

Remove the black pattern piece from the sheet and carefully remove the blended half leaf. Insert this into the cutout space in the black disk where it should fit exactly. Gently pat it into place.

STEP 5:
inlay the second half of the leaf

Repeat to inlay the second half of the leaf, but this time lay the cutout clay pattern onto the leaf green blend so that the point is in the darker area. This will alternate the light and dark on the two sides of the leaf.

STEP 6: **inlay the second leaf**

Repeat to inlay the second leaf, again alternating dark and light leaf green between the two halves. This leaf has an extra piece where the underside curls around. Cut this out from the darker leaf green of the blend.

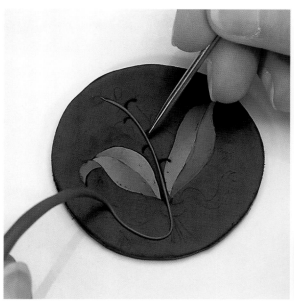

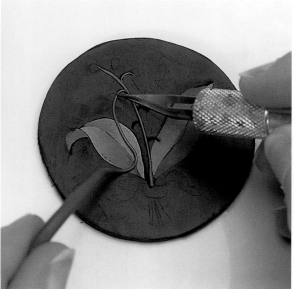

STEP 7: **inlay the stalks**

Inscribe along the lines of the stalks with the tapestry needle. Form a ⅓₂" (1mm) thick thread of leaf green (see page 15). Lay this into the inscribed grooves and pat it down.

STEP 8: **inlay the flower stalks**

Inlay the tiny flower stalks in the same way. Inlay the lower stalks below the ribbon, using pale leaf green for the two left-hand stalks to suggest that they are catching the light.

STEP 9: inlay the buds

Cut out the small buds at the top of the stem, overlapping the flower stalks slightly. Cut out the shapes in white clay. With such tiny round pieces, it is easiest to cut them out by eye rather than cut around the removed shapes. Inlay the shapes into their places in the background disk.

STEP 10: make a strip blend

Make a strip blend using white and gray (see page 18). The blend should be a smooth but steep gradient between the two colors.

STEP 11: inlay the flowers

Cut around the first flower outline, overlapping the stalk slightly, and remove the piece. Use the piece to cut out the flower from the white/gray blend, angling the blend so that the flower is white at the top left and dark at the bottom right. Repeat for the other flowers.

STEP 12: inlay the ribbon

Make a strip blend of blue and white. Cut out the ribbon shapes as before. Use the pieces to cut the shapes out of the blend with the pale side of the blend always to the left. Inlay the pieces into the background.

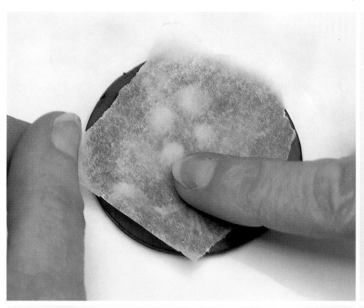

STEP 13: smooth the surface

Lay a piece of tracing paper over the pietre dure and burnish with your finger to smooth the surface. If the edges of the piece have distorted while you were working, lay the template over the piece and cut out the circle again to make the edges neat. Bake the piece on the tile for 20 minutes.

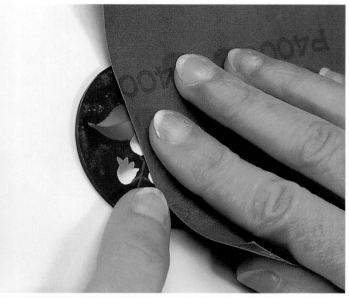

STEP 14: sand the surface

While the piece is still warm and still on the ceramic tile, hold it under a gently running faucet and sand the surface to smooth it further. Buff with fabric to give it a gentle shine.

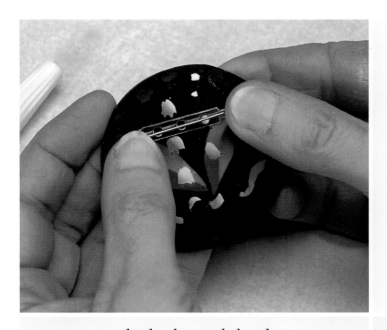

STEP 15: attach the brooch back

Glue a brooch pin to the back of the piece. If you wish, before attaching the pin, you can back the piece with another sheet of black clay cut to shape and rebake to make it thicker and more robust.

▸▸ **design your own pin:** The finished pin has a delicate beauty with the shaded flowers looking almost three-dimensional. Use other simple outlines of flowers to design your own pietre dure pieces.

I f you are an impatient person like me, then you will love making tile mosaics! These projects are quick and fun to do and are inspired by the glorious ceramic tiles that are found in cultures all over the world. People have used tiles for centuries to embellish all kinds of buildings, from the fantastic floors of medieval churches and cathedrals, to the interiors of Victorian theaters; from

tile
mosaics

humble workers' cottages, to palaces, restaurants, gardens and railway stations.

Tile mosaics usually consist of regular repeating patterns. The tiles themselves can be plain or decorated, and the tiles can be simple squares or more ornate shapes that fit together to make wonderful patterns. Plain and patterned tiles are often interspersed to add variety and interest.

Making full-size tile mosaics would involve a great deal of work, but polymer clay can be used to make beautiful miniature versions to decorate items in your home. You can either cut the shapes by hand, using a template as a guide, or use the many cutters that are available. The soft tiles can be stamped, painted, gilded, carved or decorated in any way you like!

Photocopy transfer is a method of printing permanent images onto polymer clay and is a particularly useful technique for making repeating patterns on polymer clay tiles (see page 20 for instructions). ■

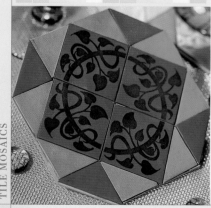

ottoman star tiles flowerpot

This project is inspired by the fabulous tiles that were made in Turkey in the sixteenth century, under the rule of the sultans of the Ottoman Empire. White clays, blue glazes and intricate flower and animal designs were combined to make tiling patterns to decorate buildings and monuments.

Here, patterned hexagonal tiles fit with simple triangles to make a six-sided star decoration for a flowerpot. The photocopy transfer technique is used to decorate the hexagonal tiles. ■

materials

- 2-ounce (or 65g) blocks of polymer clay: 1 block of turquoise, 1 block of white
- pasta machine *(or roller and wood strips)*
- ceramic baking tiles
- 4" (10cm) square terra-cotta flowerpot
- talcum powder
- ½" (13mm) triangle cutter
(or trace and cut out the triangle template provided for a pattern)
- tissue blade
- fresh photocopy of the template
(or use Lazertran Silk, see page 21)
- blue colored pencil
- matte varnish
- clear plastic triangle with ruler edge *(set square)*
- PVA glue

preparation

- **sheets:** All sheets should be rolled out to the same thickness: about ¹⁄₁₂" (2mm) or a medium setting on the pasta machine.

The pattern appears here at full size.

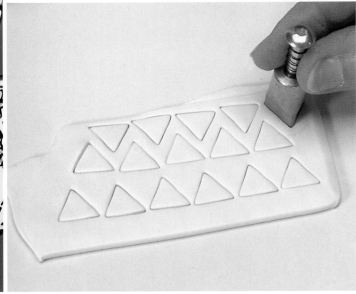

STEP 1: make the triangle tiles

Roll out the white clay about ½" (2mm) thick and lay the sheet on the ceramic tile. Dust the surface with talcum powder to prevent sticking and cut out twenty-four white triangles using the triangle cutter. If you do not have a triangle cutter, use the triangle template. Repeat with the turquoise clay to make twenty-eight turquoise triangles.

STEP 2: prepare the photocopy

(If you are using Lazertran Silk, use the instructions on page 21.) Color in the flowers on the photocopy of the template with the blue colored pencil, applying plenty of color. Cut out the hexagons just inside their outlines.

STEP 3: make the hexagon tiles

Roll out more white clay to the same thickness as before and place on a ceramic tile. Lay the four hexagons facedown onto the clay sheet and cut out your shapes, removing the waste clay. Rub the back of the paper firmly with your finger to ensure that it is in full contact with the clay. Bake all the pieces on their tiles for 20 minutes.

STEP 4: remove the paper

When the clay is cool, peel off the paper to reveal the transferred images.

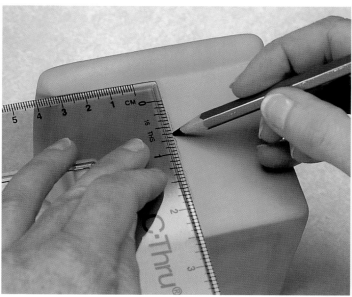

STEP 5: varnish and mark the center

Coat the outside of the pot with matte varnish to prevent the water from the soil seeping through and dissolving the glue. Use a clear plastic triangle with a ruler edge (set square) to draw a vertical guideline up the center of each side of the flowerpot.

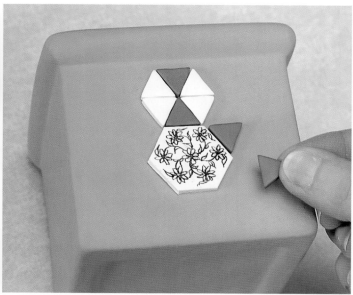

STEP 6: glue on the tiles

Working from the top of the flowerpot, glue a turquoise triangle between two white triangles in a row just below the lip of the pot. Glue a second row below the first and then a hexagon centrally below. Now glue a turquoise triangle against each side of the hexagon to make a star.

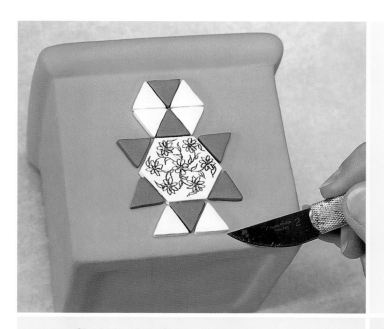

STEP 7: finish the flowerpot

Complete the pattern with two white triangles on either side of the bottom central turquoise triangle. Make sure that any horizontal edges are really horizontal and leave a small gap of about ½2" (1mm) between the tiles. Repeat to decorate the other three sides of the flowerpot.

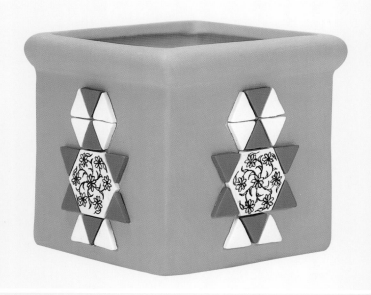

▸▸**versatile tile design:** The mellow terra-cotta of the flowerpot sets off the blue and white tiles to perfection. The tiles could be arranged in many different patterns and used to decorate all kinds of objects that have a flat surface such as picture frames, mirrors or box lids.

medieval tile coasters

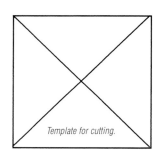

English medieval cathedrals and churches are filled with many examples of the tiler's art. This tile mosaic is based on the glorious encaustic tile designs dating from the sixteenth century that were used as cathedral floor tiles. Encaustic tiles are made by stamping a design onto a soft clay tile and then filling the impression with a different-colored clay slip. For this polymer clay version, I have simplified the process by using the photocopy transfer technique to apply the design, while copper and gold clays give a very close simulation of the originals. ■

materials

- 2-ounce (or 65g) blocks of polymer clay: 1 block of copper, 1 block of gold
- pasta machine *(or roller and wood strips)*
- ceramic baking tiles
- fresh photocopy of the template
(or use Lasertran Silk, see page 21)
- tissue blade
- thick cardboard
- craft knife
- steel ruler
- cutting mat
- PVA glue
- dark green felt

preparation

- **sheets:** All sheets should be rolled out to the same thickness: about 1/12" (2mm) or a medium setting on the pasta machine.

Template for cutting.

The pattern appears here at full size.

medieval tile coasters

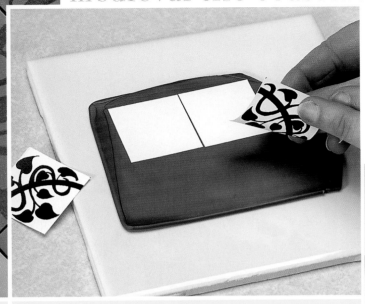

▶▶ STEP 1: **apply the photocopies**

Roll out a sheet of the copper clay about ½2" (2mm) thick and 4" (10cm)
square, and place on a ceramic tile. Cut out the photocopies of the four
patterned squares, just inside their outlines, and lay them facedown on
the clay (see page 20). Leave a slight gap between them so that you can
cut bet ween them to make the separate tiles.

STEP 2: **cut out the tiles**

Cut between the paper pieces and around the
outside with a tissue blade. Remove the waste
clay from around the tiles. (If you are using
Lazertran Silk, refer to the instructions on
page 21.)

STEP 3: **smooth down the paper**

Burnish the back of the paper with your finger to ensure that the image is
in contact with the clay over its entire surface. Otherwise, there will be
gaps in the design when you remove the paper after baking.

STEP 4: cut out the copper triangle

Use the plain paper square as a template to cut out a plain square from the copper sheet on a ceramic tile. Remove the template and cut diagonally across the clay square with your blade to quarter it into four triangles.

STEP 5: cut out the gold triangles

Roll out the gold clay in the same way and place on a ceramic tile. Use the plain square template to cut out two gold squares and quarter them as for the plain copper tiles. Bake all the pieces on their ceramic tiles for 20 minutes.

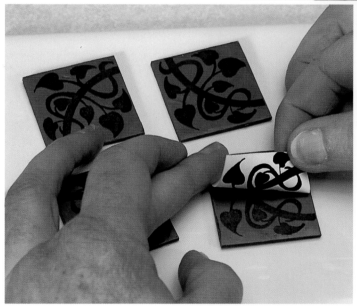

STEP 6: peel off the paper

When the tiles have cooled, peel off the paper from the patterned tiles to reveal the transferred images.

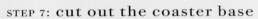

STEP 7: cut out the coaster base

STEP 8: glue the tiles to the coaster

Trace the coaster template onto thick cardboard. Cut out the shape using the craft knife, steel ruler and cutting mat.

Spread glue thinly over the cardboard and press the patterned tiles down in the central square, using the Coaster Layout below as reference. Align the tiles so that the leafy ring is formed, leaving a slight space between the tiles. Glue the gold and copper triangles around the outside.

Coaster Layout

The pattern appears here at full size.

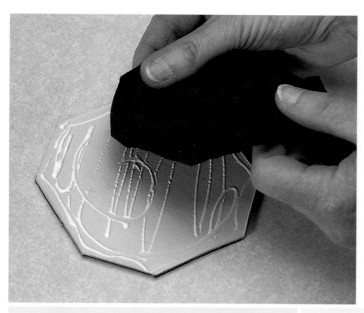

STEP 9: back the coaster with felt

Lay the coaster onto the felt, trace around it with a pen, then cut out the shape. Glue the felt to the back of the coaster, smoothing it down.

▸▸ **achieve maximum sheen:** The copper and gold colors of the finished coaster simulates medieval tiles to perfection. When using metallic or pearlescent clays, always roll them into a sheet, fold and roll again several times so that you achieve the maximum sheen.

herb fossil picture frame

Tiles have been decorated with stamped impressions for centuries, and the texture of stamped clay is very appealing. This project uses impressions of herbs to give the suggestion of fossils in natural rock for an unusual picture frame. Choose your herbs carefully; small leaves are best, and you will need a variety of shapes and sizes for the best effect. Any small plant leaves can be used as an alternative.

Choose a frame that measures in whole inches (or centimeters) if possible so that the 1" (2.5cm) square mosaic tiles fit exactly. ▪

materials

- 2-ounce (or 65g) blocks of polymer clay: 2 blocks of beige *(Premo! Ecru)*
- pasta machine *(or roller and wood strips)*
- ceramic baking tiles
- 2" (5cm) wide flat wood picture frame, approximately 12" x 10" (30cm x 25cm)
- graph paper
- darning needle
- talcum powder
- soft paintbrush
- collection of small fresh leaves: parsley, thyme, ivy, geranium, etc.
- tissue blade
- rubbing alcohol *(methylated spirits)*
- acrylic paints: dark brown, red, yellow
- fine sandpaper
- PVA glue

STEP 1: mark out the tiles

Roll out the clay into a sheet about 1/16" (1.5mm) thick, as large as possible to fit on the ceramic tile. Cover the sheet with the graph paper and prick over it at 1" (2.5cm) intervals with the needle.

STEP 2: impress the leaves

Brush a light coating of talcum powder over the clay and press the back of a leaf (or a spray) into every other square. Angle the leaves in different directions for variety. Carefully remove the leaves, using a needle to help them out of the clay if necessary.

STEP 3: cut out the tiles

Cut out the tiles with the tissue blade, aligning it along the rows of dots. Rock the blade after each cut before removing it from the clay to prevent the clay from sticking to the blade. Remove the waste clay from around the tiles. Repeat the above steps until you have made about eighty tiles. Bake the clay on the ceramic tiles for 30 minutes.

STEP 4: accentuate the impressions

When the pieces have cooled, brush over them with rubbing alcohol to degrease the surface; this will help the paint to stick. Brush dark brown paint over the leaf impressions, working the paint into the crevices.

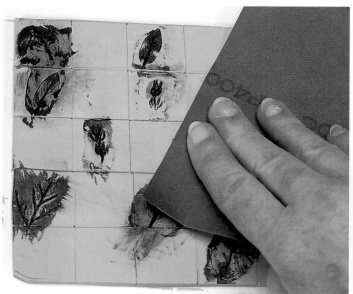

STEP 5: sand the surface

Allow the paint to dry and then sand the surface to remove most of the brown paint, leaving the residue in the leaf impressions.

STEP 6: tint the tiles' surface

Mix together yellow and red paint, diluting it to a thin orange wash. Brush this over the surface of the mosaic tiles. Keep the color variable, with red and yellow washes amongst the orange.

STEP 7: sand again

Allow the paint to dry and then sand again to make a randomly colored distressed surface. Remove the tiles from the ceramic tiles and snap them apart along the cutting lines.

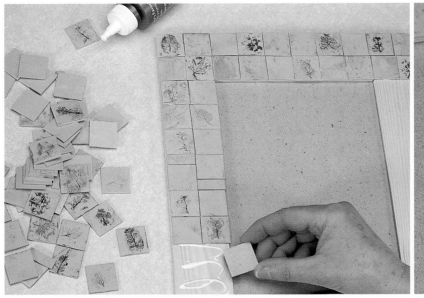

Spread glue over the top of the frame and press on the mosaic tiles, alternating the leaf tiles with plain tiles.

If the tiles do not fit the frame exactly, you will need to cut the tiles. For best effect, these should be incorporated into the design so that the bottom line consists of whole tiles. Leave the glue to dry thoroughly.

▸▸ **completed frame:** The finished frame is a glorious mix of subtle colors with delicate leafy impressions and would make a perfect surround for a family portrait. Try making the frame in a different color scheme—cool dark blues and greens impressed with silver herbs would give a beautiful effect.

resources

▶▶ polymer clay suppliers

Polymer clays are widely available in arts and crafts shops and also by mail order from craft suppliers. If you have problems finding the clays, the following suppliers should be able to help. You can also find current information on suppliers and organizations at www.heaser.co.uk.

AUSTRALIA

Rossdale Pty. Ltd.
351-353 Warrigal Road
Cheltenham 3192
Victoria
Tel: 001 613 9583 4411
E-mail: info@rossdale.com.au
Web site: www.rossdale.com.au
Premo!, Sculpey

Staedtler (Pacific) Pty. Ltd.
1 Inman Road
Dee Why NSW 2099
Sidney
Tel: 0061 2 9982 4555
E-mail: claforest@staedtler.com.au
Web site: www.staedtler.com
Fimo

CANADA

KJP Crafts
PO Box 5009 Merivale Depot
Nepean, Ontario K2C 3H3
Tel: (613) 225 6926
E-mail: kjpcrafts@attcanada.net
Web site: www.kjpcrafts.com
Premo!, Sculpey

Staedtler-Mars Ltd.
5725 McLaughlin Road
Mississauga, Ontario L5R 3K5
Toronto
Tel: (905) 501-9008
E-mail: info@staedtler.ca
www.staedtler.ca
Fimo

NEW ZEALAND

Zigzag Polymer Clay Supplies Ltd.
8 Cherry Place, Casebrook
Christchurch 8005
Tel: (+64) 3-359-2989
E-mail: sales@zigzag.co.nz
www.polymerclay.co.nz
www.zigzag.co.nz
polymer clays, tools, etc.

UNITED KINGDOM

The Polymer Clay Pit
3 Harts Lane, Wortham
Diss, Norfolk IP22 1PP
Tel: 01379 741916
E-mail: claypit@heaser.co.uk
www.heaser.co.uk
polymer clays, tools, etc.

UNITED STATES

Clay Factory of Escondido
PO Box 460598
Escondido, CA 92046-0598
Tel: (877) 728-5739
E-mail: clayfactoryinc@clayfactoryinc.com
www.clayfactoryinc.com
polymer clays, tools, etc.

American Art Clay Co., Inc.
4717 W. 16th St.
Indianapolis, IN 46222
Tel: (800) 374-1600 or (317) 244-6871
E-mail: catalog@amaco.com
www.amaco.com
Fimo

Lazertran Silk
Lists of retailers worldwide are available from:
Lazertran LTD USA
650 8th Avenue
New Hyde Park, New York 11040
Tel: (800) 245-7547
E-mail: lazertran@msn.com
www.lazertran.com

▶▶ organizations

Please send a stamped, addressed envelope when inquiring about membership.

The British Polymer Clay Guild
48 Park Close
Hethersett, Norwich NR9 3EW
UK

The National Polymer Clay Guild
Suite 115-345
1350 Beverly Road
McLean, VA 22101
USA

index

Get creative with North Light Books!

These and other fine North Light titles are available from your local art & craft retailer, bookstore, online supplier or by calling 1-800-448-0915.

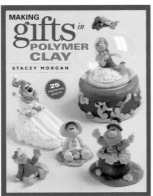

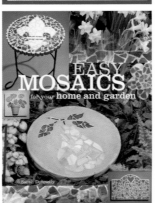

Creative Stamping in Polymer Clay

Filled with fresh designs, simple techniques and gorgeous colors, this exciting book combines two fun, easy-to-master crafts in one. You'll find guidelines for stamping images on all your clay creations, including jewelry, home décor and more, along with advice for experimenting with color and finish. The wide variety of projects guarantees spontaneous, delightful results.

ISBN 1-58180-155-6, paperback, 128 pages, #31904-K

Creative Home Decor in Polymer Clay

Now you can use polymer clay to create elegant designs for your home! Nineteen step-by-step projects make getting started easy. You'll learn how to combine clay with fabric, silverware and other household items, plus metallic powders that simulate colored glass, antique bronze or gleaming silver. You'll also find instructions for color mixing, marbling and caning.

ISBN 1-58180-139-4, paperback, 128 pages, #31880-K

Making Gifts in Polymer Clay

These twenty-one adorable projects perfectly capture the spirit of the seasons. Each one is wonderfully easy to make and simple enough to be completed in a single sitting. From leprechauns, Easter eggs and spooky witches to Thanksgiving turkeys and a polar bear on skis, there's something for everyone—including kids! You'll also find guidelines for creating magnets, buttons and pins.

ISBN 1-58180-104-1, paperback, 128 pages, #31792-K

Easy Mosaics for Your Home and Garden

You can create a range of decorative mosaics for your home and garden! These twenty exciting projects include step-by-step instructions, materials lists and templates you can enlarge and trace. There's no tile to cut and no messy grout. Just pick a project and get creative! From garden stepping stones to table tops, you'll find beautiful mosaic projects for every part of your home.

ISBN 1-58180-129-7, paperback, 128 pages, #31830-K